MW00624753

# WHAT LEADERS ARE SAYING ABOUT *ROOKIE MISTAKES* . . .

"Truly great leaders admit their mistakes, work to correct them, and share with others how to avoid them. *Rookie Mistakes* has 25 great examples that will benefit both the new leader and the veteran leader alike."

**—Marshall Goldsmith, Thinkers50 #1 Executive Coach and the only two-time #1 Leadership Thinker in the world**

"Whether it's your first leadership season or your tenth, *Rookie Mistakes* is the playbook you will want to have handy every time you step out onto the organizational 'playing field.' Mike McHargue has recruited a team of veteran leaders to tell often poignant and always powerful personal stories about their mistakes and successes and the important lessons they learned. Engaging, uplifting, and practical, *Rookie Mistakes* is a gem of a little book, and I love it."

**—Jim Kouzes, coauthor of *The Leadership Challenge*, and the Dean's Executive Fellow of Leadership, Leavey School of Business, Santa Clara University**

"So many books on leadership offer guidance on what to do to become a better leader. Mike McHargue's *Rookie Mistakes* offers us a much-needed twist: what *not* to do to get better. Whether you are a new leader or a seasoned pro, you'll return to this book again and again."

**—Ken Blanchard, coauthor of *The New One Minute Manager*® and *Servant Leadership in Action***

"Leading an organization with nearly 300,000 employees with over 2,300 different retail locations isn't always easy. Leadership mistakes are inevitable not only by rookies but also by seasoned veterans, including leaders at the very top. Mike McHargue's *Rookie Mistakes* helps highlight the most common mistakes that can cause teams to be dysfunctional and well-intentioned work to go off the tracks. This is a must-read for those wanting to avoid these common mistakes."

**—Robert (Bob) Miller, CEO and Chairman of the Board, Albertsons Companies**

"I typically have pretty low stamina for business books so really appreciated Mike McHargue's concise format and real-world stories told by an array of leaders. Learning from the mistakes of others is really impactful, and I enjoyed it!"

**—Dan Little, Chief Technology Officer, Nordstrom (retired)**

"*Rookie Mistakes* provides leaders the opportunity to learn from the mistakes and insights of others and then to reflect on their personal leadership style to avoid the same pitfalls. Strengthen your own leadership by applying the rich principles McHargue teaches in his *Rookie Mistakes*!"

**—Dee Ann Turner, Vice President (retired), Chick-fil-A, Inc. and best-selling author of *It's My Pleasure: The Impact of a Compelling Culture and Extraordinary Talent***

"In the last 7-10 years, it's been exciting to watch the business world come to the same realization that the sports world has known for decades . . . organizational health and culture matter—especially if you desire to be a champion in your industry. Mike McHargue does a masterful job of sharing 'quick hit' stories that will keep you engaged and ready to apply, regardless of your leadership experience."

**—Brent Jones, three-time Super Bowl Champion, San Francisco 49ers**

"When it comes to leadership, we're all rookies. Reading this will be a gift—not just to you, but to your team."

**—John Ortberg, senior pastor at Menlo Church and author of *I'd Like You More If You Were More Like Me***

"'Culture eats strategy for breakfast' is the only thing a rookie manager needs to know. Unfortunately, it takes experience to get there! This book can serve as a great reference for anyone in a leadership position, especially rookies. When you face the inevitable conundrum of management and people, just thumb to the page about 'that problem.' It is like having a seasoned mentor in your hands."

**—David R. Duncan, President and CEO, Silver Oak and Twomey Cellars**

"*Rookie Mistakes* is a master class in leadership that weaves together powerful storytelling with keen insights to deliver practical advice for anyone who aspires to be a better leader."

**—Chris Beard, CEO, Mozilla**

"McHargue's practical application of principles taught by The Table Group and Patrick Lencioni's organizational health concepts is a perfect reflection for all leaders trying to improve their leadership skills. McHargue leverages classic examples from proven leaders to reinforce these concepts, assisting leaders of all skill levels to reflect and learn from missteps in the challenging world of leadership. All leaders, new and experienced, can gain a tremendous amount from these five missteps and how to avoid them."

**—Jeff Feeler, Chairman and CEO, US Ecology, Inc.**

"Not just another book on leadership, this is a truly useful guide to what leaders can and should do. Critical to leadership effectiveness and building a culture of employee engagement."

**—Robert Castan, CEO, Northpoint Recovery, LLC**

"While reading my copy of *Rookie Mistakes*, I was immediately able to apply one of its many lessons to an issue with a new member of our team. It helped me support a top-notch employee and reminded me that even six years into a job, you can still make simple errors. I commend Mike McHargue for creating an excellent book through a mix of valuable advice, engaging story format, and fun executive self-assessment. I would recommend this to any leader looking to improve their skills or the health of their team."

**—Ben Bledsoe, President and CEO, Consumer Direct Care Network**

"I have hired Mike McHargue twice to work with our executive team. There are no 'trust falls' when you have a session with Mike; he gets right to work and helps you solve problems. His book is fun to read and provides key lessons for leaders of all levels."

**—Jason Goldberger, President and CEO, Blue Nile**

"*Rookie Mistakes* is a coach/mentor in itself for company leaders committed to improving organizational health."

**—Jeff LeDoux, President and CEO, Houston Engineering, Inc.**

"McHargue has done brilliant work with my company to help us learn from these lessons, and I'm so pleased to see these 'gifts' broadly available in this book. Any leader whose mind is open and curious will gain immensely from these lessons and contribute significantly to the health of their organization."

**—Chris Taylor, President and CEO, Fisher's Technology**

"I wish Mike McHargue had written this book 30 years ago when I was a 'rookie.' I found myself making notes and identified several items I need to revisit or incorporate myself and/or with my senior leadership team. An easy read with many takeaways for everyone, veteran or rookie."

**—LuAnn Bott, President and CEO, Make-A-Wish**
**Missouri & Greater Kansas City**

"In his work, Mike McHargue creates simple principles and processes to address complex challenges, and he's done it again with his book *Rookie Mistakes*. Leaders who apply its simple truths are sure to see a positive impact on their leadership tool kit and ultimately drive better results in their business."

**—Andy Heily, President, Continental Mills**

"Mike McHargue has a done a masterful job of taking his expertise and interweaving it with first-person accounts from seasoned executives across a wide variety of industries. Their stories significantly enhance the reader's understanding and accelerate practical application of the principles contained in the book."

**—Reid Stephan, VP and Chief Information Officer,**
**St. Luke's Health System**

"Mike McHargue hits the mark on the five mistakes. Each one of them affects the overall culture of the workplace and directly affects the productivity and commitment at all levels of the organization. I recommend this for any level of experienced or inexperienced leader."

**—Dan McNamara, Senior Vice President and**
**General Manager, Intel Corporation**

"*Rookie Mistakes* is a powerful leadership tool that is relevant for all leaders by focusing on critical mistakes to avoid and also on how to improve as a leader. Leaders will undoubtedly find *Rookie Mistakes* an invaluable resource they will immediately benefit from and wish they had when they started their careers."

**—Dave Gillrie, Senior Vice President, Forestry, Lawn,**
**and Garden Division, Blount International**

"*Rookie Mistakes* would be a great read for any new leader or any leader taking on a new role."

**—Kevin Riley, CEO, First Interstate Bank**

"I hate to admit it, but I see myself in all the rookie mistakes this book discusses. Unfortunately, I am not a rookie! This book is a great reminder for me, and it will go on the list of books I need to re-read every year. A great blend of theory and reality, delivered in an easy-to-read, engaging format."

**—Marty Cullen, CEO and Owner, Perfect Plumbing, Heating & Air**

"The short stories in *Rookie Mistakes* are designed to get the leader thinking about the way they lead and how they set the tone for their organization."

**—Ryan Cantrell, Superintendent, Elementary Principal, and Special Education Director, Bruneau-Grand View School District**

"Mike McHargue presents powerful insights on how leaders create clarity through the fabric of their organization, which translates directly to the bottom line."

**—Calvin Fillmore, Corporate President,
Diamond Line Delivery Systems, Inc.**

"Mike McHargue has brought together essential leadership principles with real-life stories that are relatable and illustrate the power of five critical leadership behaviors needed to dramatically improve the health of your organization."

**—Tony Bavuso, CEO, Saving Sight**

"Mike McHargue nails the essential traits of great leadership and the mistakes we should avoid. The stories are impactful and relatable. This is a must-read for freshly minted graduates and seasoned professionals."

**—Adele Oliva, Managing Partner at 1315 Capital, LLC**

"As a former client, employee, and current peer of Mike McHargue, I can attest to his ability to identify the critical leadership areas everyone needs to master. From connecting with your team to giving and receiving feedback, I've seen Mike apply the lessons shared by the very best in their industry. This will be the book I give my clients this year."

**—Al Amador, Principal Consultant, The Table Group**

"Savvy leaders and novice leaders alike will benefit from Mike McHargue's *Rookie Mistakes.* No matter what kind of leader you are, you will find yourself in one (or more!) of these stories and will appreciate the advice that sets you on the right path."

**—Aaron Howell, President and Founder, Northwest Lineman College**

"Mike McHargue speaks to the deepest human connections that leadership can forge—engaging values and vulnerability, expressing gratitude and affirmation, resolving conflict, and inspiring change."

**—Father Gerdenio Manuel, S.J., Clinical Psychologist, Professor and Director of University of San Francisco St. Ignatius Institute**

"I had the pleasure of working with Mike McHargue for over 10 years. A compassionate and empathetic leader, he is the exact right person to encourage leaders to avoid common mistakes. His *Rookie Mistakes* will inspire you to think big on your path to becoming a better leader."

**—Micaela Breber, Learning Evangelist, Large Enterprise Relationship Manager, LinkedIn**

"Throughout my career in the Navy and then in consulting and sales leadership, I endured, observed, and made most of the mistakes highlighted in this book. Today, a few years past my rookie season, I still make many of those same mistakes, which made *Rookie Mistakes* even more relevant as it gave me an opportunity to find positive and practical reminders that leadership is a fascinating journey with many lessons along the way. Regardless of your profession or career stage, you will find something in *Rookie Mistakes* that resonates."

**—Kevin Duffer, Vice President, Sales and Business Development, Management Concepts**

"Mike McHargue's access to first-rate leaders and his own hard-won wisdom and perspective make *Rookie Mistakes* essential reading for people who want to avoid these common leadership errors."

**—Mark Traylor, Founder and Executive Pastor, Eastwind Community Church**

"Having reported to Mike McHargue for nearly a decade during his early leadership days, I can confirm he made mistakes! However, not being perfect and his dedication to help me learn from his mistakes are what made him such an effective leader and what makes this book so valuable. Whether you are a rookie leader or an experienced one, you will find great value and humor in relating to many of the stories shared here."

**—Andy Pederson, Enterprise Sales Executive, Grand Rounds, Inc.**

"If you're leading, you are either making mistakes or worried about them. The humanity in these stories will give you patience with your own struggles and guidance for your growth. Read them."

**—David Ross, Ph.D., Principal Consultant, The Table Group**

"We can all place ourselves in these quick stories, with the added perspective of someone else's outcomes. A clever way to force our consideration of our own behaviors and styles."

**—Rick McClenning, National Sales Manager,
Paul Mueller Company**

# ROOKIE MISTAKES

## ADVICE FROM TOP EXECUTIVES ON 5 CRITICAL LEADERSHIP ERRORS

Mike McHargue

***Rookie Mistakes:*** *Advice from Top Executives on Five Critical Leadership Errors*
Mike McHargue © 2018



For more information, visit Mike-McHargue.com

Scott Adams Dilbert cartoons have been used with permission of ANDREWS MCMEEL SYNDICATION.

Hardcover ISBN: 978-1-61206-172-6
Softcover ISBN: 978-1-61206-173-3
eBook ISBN: 978-1-61206-174-0
Audio Book ISBN: 978-1-61206-175-7

Editor: AnnaMarie McHargue
Author Photo: Gina Marie Cafiero
Cover Design: Leslie Hertling
Interior Design: Fusion Creative Works, FusionCW.com

Published by

AlohaPublishing.com
Printed in the United States of America

To my wife, Anna, for your amazing grace
during 25 years of my mistakes.

And, to my kids, Elena, Jack, and Gabriella.
Go fast, take chances, and learn from your mistakes.
Because you know where whiners go . . .

# TABLE OF CONTENTS

## MISTAKE #2
Failing to Connect with Your Team

## MISTAKE #3
Running Truly Awful Meetings

## MISTAKE #4

## Hiring Too Fast, Firing Too Slow

## MISTAKE #5
Failing to Give and Solicit Feedback

# FOREWORD

Rookies are prone to mistakes, and we expect that. Veterans are prone to mistakes, and we are surprised by that. What Mike McHargue has done in *Rookie Mistakes* is provide a primer and a reminder all in one. What's particularly effective about what he's done here is give readers colorful and practical advice, and then reinforce that advice through the experiences of leaders who are humble enough to tell their stories.

A new leader needs wisdom, but in this age of ubiquitous information, it has become a great challenge to sift through everything that is out there and come up with something that is both relevant and digestible. McHargue has done just that. He has curated the insights he has gained in his consulting with a fascinating mix of leaders from a wide variety of fields—people who have made mistakes, learned from them, and want to help others avoid some of their missteps.

Beyond the wisdom of the concepts and stories, McHargue is a masterful communicator, combining practical insights with humor. *Rookie Mistakes* is not only a readable and useful book, it should be a resource for leaders who want access to just-in-time advice when they are staring squarely at a situation which has the potential for success or failure. So, read the advice here, and keep it handy. Even if you're a rookie, one day soon you'll be seen as a veteran, and you'll recognize that no one is immune from the occasional mistakes that are part of having the courage to be a leader.

> Patrick Lencioni
> Founder and CEO, The Table Group
> Best-Selling Business Author

# AUTHOR'S NOTE

Why five?

I have heard it said that three is a magic number. There is small, medium, and large. Gold, silver, and bronze. Red, yellow, and green. But I would argue that a better, more complete number is five.

Five is the number of aspiration. It's a five-star hotel, restaurant, or theater production. It is the highest ranking on a team assessment. It is the exact right amount—a handful. (And, really, who doesn't love a high five?) It's also a great size for a team. Large enough for diversity, but small enough to be agile and execute with speed.

And, as we try to recall things to our minds, five things come easily.

Written with all of this in mind, *Rookie Mistakes: Advice from Top Executives on Five Critical Leadership Errors* fully embraces this aspirational number: five chapters (mistakes) with five stories each. Easy to remember. Easy to apply.

It is my hope that these five chapters offer something you can use as you work to become the leader you always imagined you would be.

# INTRODUCTION

Throughout my career, both in technology organizations and now as a principal consultant focused on the organizational health movement, I have seen experienced executives and rookie leaders alike make the same leadership mistakes over and over. In fact, I made many of those same mistakes both as a junior leader and sometimes now, as a veteran leader. But I can say with conviction that many of my errors could have been avoided, had a seasoned executive or two (or, in this case, 25) offered a little advice or shared a relevant experience as I chartered those new leadership waters. I remember the day I thought some of the guidance might come.

When I started my career in management about 20 years ago, I was working as a sales manager for a software technology start-up in Silicon Valley. It was a great time to be in technology sales and a great time for start-ups—the heart of the dot.com run-up. With Y2K fears at their frenzied peak, breakthrough technologies being developed and productized, and new companies being formed daily in dorm rooms and coffee shops, there was a lot going on in that time and place in the technology world.

One day our CEO called me into his office unexpectedly. In the office already sat three additional members of his executive team, awaiting my arrival. This was going to either be really good or really bad! One of the four executives shared that our company's senior sales leader was leaving to go to another start-up called "Gogle"—that's really what he said . . . Gogle!—and wondered out loud why any person in his right mind would leave our great start-up for that little, oddly named company. (Last I heard that departing leader was living on an island somewhere—*his* island!) The executive leaders had called me into the office, hoping I would consider taking over that significant leadership role in our organization. The role meant not only that I would join the senior executive team in leading the sales and support teams, but I would also take responsibility for all customer relationships across multiple geographies. I was flattered and excited, but having never led such a large organization with multiple teams before, I was understandably nervous. I asked what I'd need to do to be successful.

Those top executives collectively looked me in the eye and spent the next several hours taking turns sharing the specifics of the thoughtful plan they had jointly crafted specifically with my success and the success of the organization in mind. It included taking an assessment geared toward helping determine my strengths and weaknesses as a leader as well as a thorough development plan I would follow to help me grow in my new role. They had set aside a significant budget for classes and coaching I might need as I learned and crafted my skills as a world-class leader. And, best of all, each of them committed to taking personal interest in my success by setting aside time, each week, to mentor me. The intent of the mentoring was to provide guidance, a venue for open dialogue, and to help me learn from mistakes they had made or seen made in the past. With a generous pay package and equity position offered and their insistence that I take an all-expense-paid trip with my wife to Tahiti to consider their offer, I gave them each a big bear hug and left the office excited about what the future would hold.

Unfortunately, it really didn't happen that way.

Those senior executives really *did* call me into the office and offer me the job that day. But there was no personally crafted plan, no assessment to gauge my readiness, no resources set aside to help me learn and grow, and definitely no commitment to meet with me and mentor me as I took on this role. The stories of the mistakes they made were never shared, and I was left to figure the job out on my own. In response to my inquiry regarding how to be successful, one of them said, "It's really not that hard. You are selling more than everyone else; just have everyone do what you do, and we'll be in great shape." That was the extent of the training and coaching I received. So, armed with that minimal guidance—and that guidance alone—I was left to flounder through my first significant leadership role.

As a result of the lack of direction and support, and my "trial and error" approach to leadership, I made a lot of mistakes as a new leader. I cringe to think that most of those early errors could have been avoided, had I been offered even the most basic guidance. Some of the mistakes I made included allowing confusion to reign in my organization by not being clearer about purpose and priorities; failing to admit my mistakes and apologize when I made them; failing to trust the people who worked for me to do their jobs; hiring too fast and firing too slow; running truly boring meetings; and failing to give honest and direct feedback. And that's just a small sampling of my many errors.

But I wasn't all bad. There were two things I did right, early and often throughout my career as a leader, that thankfully prevented even more errors. The first was actively seeking out guidance from leaders I respected. The guidance I received, both on things I should do as a leader and things I shouldn't, often came in the form of stories. These stories brought the coaching to life, helping me grasp the importance of the guidance and how it might be applied to the teams I was leading. It also gave me an idea for a book . . . this book.

The other thing I did right as a young leader was read every book I could find on the topic of leading teams and leading people. To be clear, I am not a voracious reader. My attention span is short, and my patience for long-winded theories and thoroughly explained research methodologies is minimal. That said, in my early career as a leader, I read (or more accurately, started!) hundreds of books on this topic. But when all was said and done, the books that resonated with me most (and the ones I actually finished!) over those two decades were the fables written by Patrick Lencioni.

When I took on multiple sales teams, I read *The Five Dysfunctions of a Team.* After reading the story and applying what I learned, two things happened. First, the teams started getting along better. And, as nice as that was, more importantly, my teams' results started to improve. Dramatically. When I joined a company that was known for its terrible meetings, I read Lencioni's work *Death by Meeting* and applied what I learned across the division of the organization I led. Meetings improved because we were talking about the most important things, engaged in good debate, made better decisions, and ended each meeting with clarity. Productivity at those meetings increased, as it did across the company, as many other sub organizations also adopted that specific and practical meeting approach.

And later in my career, when I took on responsibility for a consulting business unit in my company, I read and applied the concepts from Lencioni's book *Getting Naked.* The result? Customer service scores improved, as did all of our other key performance indicators. These books and others fueled my passion for improving teams and organizations and proved that a thoughtful, disciplined approach to applying simple concepts and ideas could dramatically improve organizational results.

After leading organizations and teams for the better part of two decades, I founded my own consulting business and simultaneously aligned my business to The Table Group, a Patrick Lencioni company, working with that business as a Principal Consultant. This business and role have afforded me the opportunity to work with hundreds of CEOs and other executive leaders and their teams over the past several years. It turns out those leaders also made mistakes. Included here are many of their stories and what they learned from them. The best leaders admit their mistakes so that others might learn from them. This makes everyone on the team and in the organization better.

Whether you are a first-time manager or a seasoned executive wanting to continue to hone your skills, I am hopeful that in these pages you'll find some wisdom to help you grow as a leader.

# MISTAKE #1

## ALLOWING CONFUSION

TINA, I NEED YOU TO WRITE A COMPANY "ORIGIN STORY." ALL THE COOL COMPANIES HAVE THEM.
WHY?
Dilbert.com DilbertCartoonist@gmail.com
WHY? WELL, FOR STARTERS, WE NEED IT FOR VARIOUS THINGS. AND SO ON.
4-18-14 ©2014 Scott Adams, Inc./Dist. by Universal Uclick
I DON'T THINK I CAN BE ANY CLEARER.
I DON'T THINK YOU CAN EITHER.

# ALLOWING CONFUSION

When I work with executive teams, early in the first day together I often lead an interactive exercise called "best team" where I ask each executive to think about the best team they have ever been on. I ask that they be creative and think about teams outside of their current team and not limit their example to only business teams. Their best teams could be within their current organization or a previous employer but could also be from community organizations, schools, sports teams, churches, or even their families.

I say, "Of all the teams you have been on, in all the organizations you have worked with or for, pick the *one* team that stands out as the very best. And why *that* team? What are the things that make that particular team rise above the dozens, if not hundreds, of other teams you have worked on or for?" I give them a few minutes to come up with that best team and to note the key qualities or characteristics that made that team so great.

After a minute or two of individual reflection, I typically pair them up and ask them to share their best teams with their assigned partner. As the sharing begins, the energy in the room immediately grows exponentially. The member of the pair who is sharing the best team story sits up straighter and breaks into a smile. There is typically laughter and excitement in the room that wasn't there previously. I ask them to switch roles after a couple minutes and again there is an energy surge as the second member of each pair begins to recall their very best team. As I try to move on from this part of the exercise, invariably the conversations continue, and I need to ask multiple times for the stories to stop so we can move on. Leaders like talking about their best teams!

I run this exercise for two reasons: to set the positive tone for the off-site event and, more importantly, to start making the business case for the importance of great teams and great teamwork.

Next, I'll spend a few minutes asking for a handful of volunteers to repeat their stories for the benefit of the group. I chart their shared comments regarding the characteristics and behaviors that made those teams so great.

More often than not, the first team member to share the best team story with the larger group shares that their best team was one where politics ran rampant, confusion reigned, and that their best team had absolutely no idea about its purpose, values, goals, or top priorities.

I kid.

Instead, the first to respond explains that the very best teams had clarity of purpose in the organization or team, as well as clarity regarding values and appropriate behaviors. Goals and objectives were well defined and discussed often and, within those goals, the most important of those were both clear and repeated often by the leader to avoid confusion and a lack of team alignment.

As leaders, it is our job not only to establish clarity but to communicate that clarity, especially with respect to company purpose, values, and priorities. And we need to do that as frequently as possible. But, if truth be told, many leaders are terrible at this.

And, over the course of my career as a leader, I have been as bad as anyone. My work with leaders and their teams, though, has validated that I am not alone in some of these (weak but honest) excuses for not communicating clarity.

- I didn't know the answers or wasn't clear myself
- I was too busy to stop and share with my team/organization
- I assumed the team (somehow magically!) already knew
- I was embarrassed to repeat myself—I had smart people on my team and had told them once—surely they understood the message the first time!

These are embarrassing and inadequate reasons for allowing confusion as a leader. If you see yourself in any of these, you are in good company.

When my peers at The Table Group and I work with leaders and their teams, we work to help our clients establish both behavioral alignment as well as intellectual alignment. Based upon Patrick Lencioni's Second Discipline of Organizational Health, spelled out in *The Advantage*, we help teams answer the following six critical questions:

1. **Why do we exist?**
2. **How will we behave?**
3. **What do we do?**
4. **How will we succeed?**
5. **What is most important, right now?**
6. **Who does what?**

The idea is that if a team can answer these questions, are perfectly aligned around those answers, and are in sync behaviorally as well, the organization is on a great path toward stronger organizational health—and organizational results will follow.

So, the first mistake I address here concerns allowing confusion to reign in their teams and organizations. What follows in this section are five great leaders describing mistakes they made and advice they can share with respect to clarity in their organizations.

We begin with a story concerning the "why" of an organization—an organization's core purpose.

## ALLOWING CONFUSION ABOUT PURPOSE

David Griffin, CEO, Griffin Communications

***Breaking** News. Tornado Warning. We interrupt our regularly scheduled programming for this severe weather update.*

These alerts are broadcasted regularly from our television stations in Tulsa and Oklahoma City, Oklahoma, in April, May, and June.

As those words are said by the meteorologists and news anchors who are front and center as the spokespeople for each unfolding weather event, a flurry of activity is already taking place in our stations and across the state. Our internal company messaging system deploys to our employees, notifying them to come into the station, although most are already on their way. It's all hands on deck. Warning lights indicating breaking news are lighting up at our stations to notify all of the gravity of the situation and drive appropriate action. Storm chasers, news crews, and camera operators quickly depart and position themselves strategically but safely. This is a major weather event, and the people of our state are counting on us for timely, accurate information.

This is who we are, and this is our time.

Our company purpose is "to keep Oklahomans safe, informed, and entertained" and a crisis like this is a great and dramatic example of why we are in business. There is great clarity around this purpose both on our leadership team and across the company.

But it wasn't always this way.

Our 108-year-old company was once divided into two distinct businesses: food manufacturing and a television station in Oklahoma City. Clearly, there was no synergy at all between those two. And, even though both were strong and profitable, they were very different in purpose and focus. This not only confused people in the organization and ownership, but it also led to challenges for our leadership and their teams.

A critical point in our company's history came when we made the decision to identify the one business we wanted to be in, to split off the other business (in this case, the food side), and to articulate the purpose of our organization. We focused our energies to determine the purpose of the company and eventually crafted a message that our employees and constituents could endorse and appreciate. We believe our clear purpose is to keep Oklahomans safe, informed, and entertained.

Employees in every organization want to know the work they do has meaning. As the leadership team of our company, it is our job to define our company's purpose and to make sure our employees understand that purpose. My senior leaders and I use the "safe, informed, and entertained" statement to open every presentation, both internally and externally, and talk about it regularly in meetings across our enterprise. It informs our strategy, helps guide our decision-making, and helps us attract the right people to Griffin.

I can't emphasize enough the importance of clearly identifying the business you are in, creating an accurate and clear purpose statement, and communicating that purpose regularly across your organization.

Once my leaders and team recognized and embraced this strategy and purpose, it was much easier for us all to work together to achieve our mission of keeping our fellow Oklahomans safe, informed, and entertained.

## ALLOWING CONFUSION ABOUT VALUES

Erik Peterson, CEO, Corporate Visions, Inc.,
author of *Three Value Conversations*

**Twenty** years ago, I received what I still consider the greatest honor of my professional career. It was an award called the Founder's Award, and it was given each year to the employee who best represented the company's values.

What made this award so special was that it was *not* bestowed by management. It was voted on by employees. Prior to the ceremony, everyone in the company submitted one name and the person who got the most votes won the award.

I was not expecting that person to be me. I'd only been with the company a short time, and although we'd had a great year and I was excited to be there, it was my first year. I was just happy to be sitting there, watching from the audience as one person after another was called up on stage and recognized for various accomplishments.

The Founder's Award was the biggest honor, so it was the final award of the night. And they didn't announce the winner right away. The company founder built suspense by talking about the person who was being honored. When he finally did reveal my name, I was shocked. I somehow found myself on stage being handed a Rolex watch with an inscription on the back that read "Founder's Award Winner" and fumbling my way through a short acceptance speech.

I don't remember the actual words I spoke. What I remember is my wife in the audience, crying, because it was such a special moment. I remember being surrounded by people, my peers, hugging and congratulating me. And I remember how overwhelming and moving the whole experience was.

After the ceremony, I went out with a group of colleagues to continue the celebration. At some quiet moment late in the evening, I found myself alone in a corner of the bar. I took off the watch to look at it again. I held it in my hands, then turned it over to re-read the inscription. And as I was sitting there looking at the words, "Founder's Award Winner," it suddenly struck me that even though my fellow employees had voted me most worthy of winning this award, and even though that meant I was the person who best represented the company's values, I had *no earthly idea what any of those values were.*

I knew there were six, because I had been told there were six. I knew one was probably "teamwork," because that's always a value. I knew one must have been "vision," because I remembered a poster up on a wall somewhere of a person looking across an ocean, so of course that must have represented vision, right? But I had no idea what any of the other values were. And that's because, during that entire year when I was supposedly embodying them, those values—whatever they were—never influenced a single decision I'd made. There was no point at which I said to myself, "I've got to make this tough decision; what do the company values tell me I should do?"

Then I reflected on the effort the founders must have put in to come up with those values. There had probably been a workshop at a retreat somewhere, where they spent several days putting all these values together in the hope they would help employees make better decisions. Yet there I was, the guy who'd won the award, and those values hadn't impacted my decisions at all.

That realization stuck with me for a long time. If you don't have a good way to communicate values, why have them? Values aren't supposed to be just slogans. They're only important if they inform decision-making, and they can only be called values if you're willing to sacrifice some pretty big things to live by them. And if that's what you want your values to do, then they need to be something you can recall in the moments when you're making those tough decisions.

I told myself then that if I ever had the opportunity, I'd do a better job of getting those values across than our founders had.

Fast-forward 20 years. Now I was an executive in a different company, in a session with a consultant developing our company values. As the leadership team struggled through the exercises, listing the characteristics of our top employees and trying to translate those qualities into our core values, I felt an overpowering sense of déjà vu. Nobody outside that room knew those were the values we expected them to live by. If we were going to make them work, it wasn't enough simply to *tell* people those were our values. We had to bring them to life, in a way they'd remember, so those values would be the first thing they'd call upon when faced with tough decisions.

Here's what we did:

- We knew from our research that people remember stories better than words or slogans. So I talked to the entire company about our core values and shared real stories of team members living those values.
- Senior leaders followed up on my company-wide presentation by meeting with smaller teams of employees to share their stories and solicit examples from their own teams.

The approach worked well. Because every employee not only heard about our core values, but heard them communicated in a way that stuck, people were able to understand and act on them.

Today, as our company CEO, I am the key champion and guardian of our core values. I talk about them at every opportunity; we use them in interviewing and recruiting; we are willing to lose money, if necessary, to honor those values; and we will not hesitate to move people out of the business who do not respect or uphold them.

That's how our values inform our decision-making and guide our behavior. And that's how they make our business stronger.

---

## ALLOWING CONFUSION ABOUT GOALS

Dave Myers, CEO, Apex Leaders

**Coronado** High School in San Diego, California, has been known for its water polo teams for a long time. Anyone who cares about the sport has at least heard of this school as it has won 16 regional championships and three state championships since 1999, has had consecutive representation on every U.S. Olympic water polo team in the five Olympic games up to and including 2016, and has had a 100 percent acceptance rate into the U.S. Navy Seals program over the past few decades. No other school can claim that same success on *any* of those metrics, much less all four. Years ago, I was fortunate to be able to play for that team.

During those precious high school years, though, I had no idea how the success of that team and the lessons I learned there would mold me as a future leader. At the time, I didn't fully understand the impact of putting team over self as we worked toward a common goal. Or that success came when you combined hard work and the correct execution of small mechanics of the game. Or that our wins and losses ultimately came from holding each other accountable for our actions and efforts.

After high school, I went on to play college water polo at U.C. Berkeley. And, while that team had a collection of amazing athletes, it didn't achieve anywhere near the same type of success our high school team had achieved. Our challenges as a team came alongside our relative lack of focus, a failure to put our shared goals above that of the individual, and limits to really holding one another accountable.

These failures followed me into the business world. Lack of focus and a misunderstanding about company goals and objectives were evident across many of these companies in my early career. Goals and objectives for individual team members were never as clear as they should have been, so no one was accountable for the company's misses or successes. Predictably and sadly, those companies had intermittent success and, in most cases, great potential that was never realized. When I look back on those organizations, especially those where I had a leadership role, it has become clear that I was part of the problem. It is a leader's job to create clarity around goals, get buy-in from the team, ensure accountability, and ultimately deliver results.

As I crafted a business plan to launch my own company, Apex Leaders, I vowed not to follow that same pattern of poor focus, lack of understanding, and missed opportunity. I take every opportunity—and make others—to ensure that we have great clarity about the direction our company is headed.

Six years ago at Apex Leaders, we developed a new process to ensure we were aligned in our thinking. First, we set three-year goals to lay out a big picture. We followed that with one-year goals that were broken into quarterly 13-week "sprints" with designated individuals who were responsible for carrying a specific goal—what we called rocks. Related to these rocks, we gave very specific assignments to each team member who was then responsible for ensuring commitments were met. Every rock was measured in a simple manner of red, yellow, or green. Asking, "What's our green on that?" was a concise way of asking what success would look like on a defined goal. Daily monitoring of key metrics (via dashboards) and weekly team meetings, where we reviewed the prior week's progress on the three or four rocks we had for a quarter, ensured friendly accountability; we made sure each rock received the attention and focus it deserved. If a rock was in danger of not being met (color coded red) it got the extra attention and the resources it deserved to get back on track. And finally, to ensure we weren't overtaken by distractions, we tied bonuses to the accomplishment of each quarterly and annual goal. When it came to setting goals, we learned less is more—laser focus on a few key objectives was the trick. The team had to get comfortable saying "no" more often than it said "yes" to goals it wanted to achieve.

Using this process, Apex Leaders has consistently achieved its annual objectives and has multiplied the business 10x over the last six years. We then set a subsequent goal to 10x the business in the next six years. While growing exponentially, the company received annual community recognition for being one of the best places to work. I am convinced that none of this would have happened without intense focus or without the alignment and clarity around goals and objectives that my team and I live daily.

## ALLOWING CONFUSION ABOUT PRIORITIES

Dennis Doan, Fire Chief, City of Boise

**It** was the evening of June 30, 2016, when I received an emergency notification from headquarters. My wife and I turned to each other and simultaneously said, "I smell fire." Duty was calling, and I had to get to the incident command post (ICP) immediately. As I left home with appropriate urgency, my wife asked me for the first of many times that evening if she needed to evacuate. I told her to stay put, at least for now. As I drove away I could see the line of fire in the foothills, approximately two miles from my house. The fire would become known as the "Table Rock Fire" and would eventually burn over 2,500 acres in a five-hour period.

For the 300 people who make up our department, a fire in our hometown is always personal. In this instance the proximity to my home, family, and neighbors made this one all the more so.

When I arrived at the ICP, the battalion chief was leading the response and in command. It was a joint effort with the Bureau of Land Management, an effort that would deploy over 200 firefighters, 14 structure engines, 20 wildland engines, two hot shot crews, a dozer, and numerous air assets before the night was over. As per protocol, he would command the effort from start to finish. My role was to support his work, provide guidance, aid in the big decisions as needed, and be the point person for informing the mayor, the city council, the public, and the media via interviews and regular timely updates. Decisions would need to be made quickly and the stakes were high. As is often the case for our line of work, this was truly a matter of life or death.

With 50-mile-per-hour winds and the fire moving in the direction of thousands of foothill homes, a first and most critical decision was whether we would conduct a direct attack and aggressively fight the fire and shelter in place or conduct an indirect attack by evacuating first and containing the fire second.

With limited time to make this critical decision, we looked to our three strategic priorities during a crisis like this:

1. Life safety
2. Incident stabilization
3. Property conservation

Using those priorities as strategic anchors to make the decision, we decided to aggressively fight the fire. This meant *not* evacuating. In a fire crisis like this, you have to choose to go on offense *or* play defense—there isn't time or resources to do both. In taking the offensive strategy, we immediately put the men and women of our department in the actual line of the fire between the homes and the encroaching blaze. This strategy and their great execution of the strategy worked successfully: the fire was diverted around the homes in danger and was eventually put out completely.

It turned out to be the right decision. The evening fire had started with the potential of thousands of homes lost and the potential of many lives lost as well. Once the fire was out, only two structures were lost and no human casualties.

I credit the success of this night to the brave men and women of our department working in tandem with those of the Bureau of Land Management. What enabled their success was that priorities were clear and proper protocols were followed.

Obviously, priorities are critical and must be clear when a crisis is at hand, but what about when the urgency is not so great, and life is not at risk? I would contend that it is critical then as well. Leaders shouldn't wait for a fire (a literal one or a figurative one) to know what's most important. Those priorities should be stack-ranked and at the top of everyone's mind.

In our department, I have made sure our priorities were also clear with respect to appropriate behaviors. Our core values of "trust" and "selfless service" were in the thoughts of every man and woman in our department in *every one* of the over 30,000 calls we have received on average, every year. These values have guided our decision-making and approach to handling each of those calls with personal attention and care.

Clarity of priorities in crisis, with respect to behaviors (core values) and with respect to the goals of our department, has informed our decisions, aligned our leaders and teams, and made sure we delivered on our promise—our core purpose of "protecting lives, property, and the environment."

---

## ALLOWING CONFUSION BY UNDER-COMMUNICATING

Beth Toal, Vice President, Communications and Marketing, St. Luke's Health System

Of all people, I know the importance of sharing messages multiple times (research says at least seven!) before people actually internalize your point. As the Vice President for Communications and Marketing for the largest healthcare system in Idaho, two of my primary responsibilities are to articulate the mission of our organization, which is "to improve the health of the people in the communities we serve," and to communicate the organization's ICARE values, which are "integrity," "compassion," "accountability," "respect," and "excellence" to those communities. My department's role in the organization is to "communicate and activate the mission of St. Luke's" and that begins with consistent and clear external messaging.

So, how was it possible that I missed the mark communicating with my own team?

My team is extremely competent and professional, and many have worked together for years. However, at one point, I started to recognize that something was off. It felt like team members were working in silos, and it was becoming increasingly difficult to get things finished. I started noticing increased bickering and infighting where there had been none before. I found myself having to intervene more and more. Significant time in my meetings and sometimes the better parts of my day were spent mediating misunderstandings and personal conflicts.

On top of that, when we would get together for leadership meetings and someone on the team would ask a question, I would be thinking, *Haven't we already had this conversation?* I couldn't figure out why things were no longer "clicking."

That's when the irony struck me. While my team and I were doing a good job communicating externally, I assumed I was doing that same good job communicating internally. That hadn't been the case. My internal team needed more from me. They needed me to communicate clearly and constantly.

Once that realization struck me, I knew I couldn't simply solve this with a one-time communication meeting. I needed to be intentional about *over-communicating*. If I didn't add this intention, I would slip back into muscle memory and do exactly what I had been doing previously. My challenge was to ensure I didn't let that happen again. I didn't want to take for granted that we would figure things out without constant communication of a clear message across the department.

After multiple senior leadership meetings with my direct reports to create and reinforce clarity around the most important things, we held the first of what became many department-wide meetings to clarify and reinforce our purpose, discuss living our values, plan together how we would succeed going forward, and communicate the top priorities in the department. We blew up our meeting structure and started over in how meetings and communication would flow. As a team, we committed to discuss the most important things with the right people in the right venues *at the right frequency*. We recognized our differences with respect to managing conflict and have used that new understanding to ensure healthy and constructive conversations. This, we believed, would ensure we didn't slip back into the old behaviors that resulted in poor or ineffective communication as had plagued us months earlier.

Effective, clear communication took discipline and regular auditing and improvement to ensure it stayed effective for my team. As a result of our deliberate work in this area, my leaders and the rest of the department again began performing at their highest levels. Communication—indeed over-communication—began flowing up, down, and across the department, and achievement of our aggressive work plan was well within reach.

---

# LEADER SELF-ASSESSMENT

Please rate yourself as you believe your team members would rate you on the following skills and talents by choosing the appropriate number from the terms below. Then total the numbers to see your overall self-assessment for this category.

| LOUSY | NEEDING TO IMPROVE | OK | PRETTY GOOD | OUTSTANDING |
|---|---|---|---|---|
| 1 | 2 | 3 | 4 | 5 |

**Do I allow confusion?**

_______ 1. My team would say I am __________ at communicating the company's purpose.

_______ 2. My team would say I am __________ at communicating the company's values.

_______ 3. My team would say I am __________ at communicating the company's and team's goals.

_______ 4. My team would say I am __________ at communicating the company's and team's priorities.

_______ 5. My team would say I am __________ at continuously communicating the most important things in our business.

_______ **Confusion total**

---

23+ = Outstanding—this is a real strength for you
18–22 = Pretty good—you are on your way to greatness
13–17 = OK—not bad (but do you really want to be an average leader?)
8–12 = Needing to improve—you have some work to do
5–7 = Lousy—this is a real challenge for you and therefore, for your team

# MISTAKE #2

## FAILING TO CONNECT WITH YOUR TEAM

BEFORE I MAKE MY DECISION, I'D LIKE TO ASK FOR YOUR OPINIONS.
IT'S SUPPOSED TO MAKE YOU FEEL "ENGAGED."
AND YOU ACTUALLY PLAN TO LISTEN TO US?
I'M HOPING IT WILL LOOK THAT WAY ON THE OUTSIDE.
Dilbert.com DilbertCartoonist@gmail.com
12-19-12 ©2012 Scott Adams, Inc./Dist. by Universal Uclick

# FAILING TO CONNECT WITH YOUR TEAM

Years ago, shortly after being promoted into my first true executive position with a technology company, I attended my initial senior leadership team meeting. I was young, full of energy and what I thought were good ideas and opinions. I walked into that meeting ready to make a difference by contributing to the meeting and to the important issues facing our company.

It was the CEO's weekly meeting, and he was one of the smartest guys I had ever worked with. He had been a key strategist on defining our market, which ensured we had an early leadership position as the market developed. He had secured investors, hired a number of really smart people who were excited to help this young company achieve its potential, and followed his strategy closely. And while his cup overflowed with smarts and great strategic approaches and ideas, that cup didn't have any space left in it for other important personal leadership qualities such as openness, transparency, and vulnerability. This leader lacked humility. He was the smartest one in the room, every room, and wanted to make sure everyone knew it.

This meeting began, as was the custom, with a monologue that had something to do with what he had done particularly well or an impressive new idea that he had come up with. As he made his opening remarks, though, he said something that I disagreed with. Being young, a bit naïve, and wanting to make my mark on the team and company, I spoke up and challenged his comment. I said, "That's not true, I have to disagree."

As soon as those fateful words hit the air, every head in the room turned my direction. Clearly, I had shocked the whole lot by challenging our brilliant leader. The whole team braced themselves for the explosion that was about to follow. They had been to this "movie" before and had not given fair warning to their new junior executive peer.

The CEO struck fast and immediately began dressing me down, belittling me in front of the group, and going on with some stamina as to why he was right and I was wrong. His tirade sent the absolutely clear message to me and the others: "Don't you *dare* ever challenge me in front of this team." Believe me it was an error I wasn't about to repeat.

One of my peers, the VP of Marketing, pulled me aside after we walked out of the meeting and said, "We don't *do that* in there." After thanking him for that obvious insight and sharing that it would have been nice to know that *before* the meeting, he went on: "If you want to keep your job (I did; I had only had the job about a week), I'd suggest you don't do that again."

The message from the CEO to me and the others on our team that day was clear. He was in no way going to show any vulnerability—and we shouldn't either. The ramifications of his lack of vulnerability went far beyond this one moment of embarrassment for a young leader, though. It taught every single one of us that we should never show weakness, never ask for help, and ensured that we would stay in our respective lanes. It created a siloed atmosphere in the company at the most senior level that cascaded throughout our business. A culture of advocacy rather than collaboration was created and cemented. When challenges arose across the enterprise, there was no help requested, no help given. Small, solvable problems became bigger, less manageable ones and eventually led to the collapse of the company.

If you were to read the obituary of that company, it would convey that we had strategy problems, product issues, sales troubles, and financial irregularities—all true. But those are all things I *know* we had the smarts to solve early on, had our leadership team shared them and worked through them together. The lack of vulnerability demonstrated by the leader, the lack of relationships and teamwork on the executive team that ensued, and therefore, the lack of help we gave one another ensured that our small problems would grow into unmanageable ones. Relatively quickly, our young company, which initially showed such great promise, imploded.

This lack of vulnerability/humility is one way leaders can fail to connect to the people they lead, and I've seen, multiple times, the negative consequences of those mistakes.

What follows are five examples of the "failure to connect" mistake along with recommendations from five great (and vulnerable!) leaders who were willing to share them.

## LACKING VULNERABILITY

Dr. William Morice, II, President, Mayo Medical Laboratories and Department Chair, Laboratory Medicine and Pathology, Mayo Clinic

**Physicians** are not known for their vulnerability. As a senior leader in one of the most respected research healthcare organizations in the world, I should probably cite research that supports this statement, but I think vulnerability is a tough thing to measure. However, my own qualitative research—looking at myself in the mirror first and also talking to peers and colleagues during my 24 years as a leader, researcher, and practitioner—supports that statement.

While I can't cite published research, I *can* share an expert opinion relevant to this story and the organization I lead, shared with me by Dr. Richard Boyatzis. Dr. Boyatzis is an expert in organizational emotional intelligence who has worked extensively with academic medical centers. Of the medical professions he has worked with, he has found that pathologists, surgeons, and radiologists are the three groups most resistant to change, likely due to their high reliance on data-driven cognitive pathways. As the leader responsible for both the department of pathology as well as Mayo Medical Labs, a fast-paced, ever-changing business enterprise within the Clinic, this presents a real challenge. I suspect the reason for this general lack of vulnerability within these physician specialties is that these professionals confuse vulnerability with competence. The risks to incompetence are often high for these doctors, sometimes life or death. Can you be a good leader who is both vulnerable *and* competent?

I've learned over the course of my career as a leader, though, that vulnerability is a key trait in leadership excellence. In the work my senior leadership team did with The Table Group, not only did we learn about vulnerability-based trust, but we put into practice what we learned. The outcome during our work together at our first off-site and since has been better, more open conversations, greater debate, and ultimately better decisions for our organization. Although it may sound "touchy-feely" (and I always worry that my academic colleagues will think that), on the contrary it is anything but. This trait, which I try to model for my senior leaders and encourage across our departments, has led to improved business outcomes, increased employee engagement, and, most importantly, better patient care—the primary reason the Mayo Clinic exists.

But saying we are going to be vulnerable and actually doing so are still challenges. I am far from perfect at this. In fact, my ability to demonstrate vulnerability in the midst of change was put to the test recently during a business change initiative I hoped to implement. For weeks I worked on a presentation about this new initiative in hopes of getting buy-in from the senior executive team I report to. The meeting went well, and the executives offered their support. I was thrilled with the decision and excited about the prospect of sharing this news with my team. I expected they would be supportive and ready to jump in to make it happen.

But that's not how they responded.

Few of my leaders and their teams knew much about the initiative. I hadn't briefed them in detail, and I hadn't asked for their opinions or advice. Rather, I had inadvertently excluded them from the process. So, while I was thrilled that the initiative was supported by the executives, I realized it meant little if my team hadn't bought in and committed to the initiative's success. In my excitement, I had skipped this important step. I had made a leadership error and needed to find a way to recover. Though I could have denied the mistake, forced the issue, and demanded support, this was not the kind of leader I wanted to be. After all, hadn't we agreed to be vulnerable and honest with one another?

I immediately began setting up meetings across the department's divisions to admit my mistake, make a proper and thorough case for the new initiative, and ask for their help, buy-in, and support.

Although it was an example of "better late than never," it appears my team appreciated my honesty and vulnerability. The approach and apology addressed their concerns and lessened their resistance to the forthcoming change. They gave me their support, and we are now aligned around the new initiative, which is key to the future success of the business. Leading indicators as the change initiative is implemented point to a more successful long-term business based on these changes.

My hope is that this vulnerability-based approach to leadership will be a legacy I leave at the Mayo Clinic and with the people I have led during my career.

---

## NOT GETTING TO KNOW YOUR TEAM

Chris Cohen, Sales Leader, LinkedIn

I played basketball at Seattle Pacific University for a coach named Jeff Hironaka. He was not only the best coach I have ever had but one of the best leaders I have ever known. From an X's and O's perspective he knew the game as well as anyone and was a great practice and game manager, but that is not what set him apart from other coaches. His real gift as a coach and leader was the authentic care he showed for his players. He got to know us personally, took great interest in our development as players and as people, and always put the team goals and his players' goals ahead of his own. As a direct result of this approach, we worked harder and achieved greater success as a team, as student athletes and, eventually, as business professionals than we would have otherwise.

When I took my first leadership position for Gallo Wine Company, you would think I would have immediately followed his lead, but I didn't.

Upon taking the position as a district manager, I immediately got out in the field to survey accounts and begin assessing how well individuals on the team were doing in preparation for my first team meeting. In one of my first store visits, two of my team members were actually in the store at the time, building a large wine display in the front lobby. I walked in and said a quick hello to my two new reps and then jumped right into business by pulling out my clipboard, making my way around the store, and filling out our standard survey form. I had failed to spend even two minutes connecting with these two direct reports or pause to think this would be a good time to build rapport. Even worse, I didn't ask if they needed help building their display. I was much more focused on how I was establishing myself in my new position and having these reps see my new of level of importance. Through their lens, I have no doubt, they were thinking I was nothing more than a six-foot-seven-inch jackass.

It didn't take me long in that position to realize that my approach was a poor one. First impressions are important in any relationship, especially as a new leader. Although I worked to repair the relationships soon after, a lot of damage was done. It took me a while to recover from that initial error.

This early mistake has been a constant point of reflection for me as I have taken on new, progressively larger leadership roles, first within the consumer-packaged goods industry and then the SAAS tech industry. Channeling Coach Hironaka's approach in getting to know his team members and building foundational relationships is the first thing I work toward now when I take on a new role with a new team, or when on-boarding a new team member. I want to know each of them as a whole person, not just their professional side. What excites them about life? What motivates them and gets them up in the morning? What weighs on them and is holding them back from achieving their best selves? My ultimate question early on with a new team member is *How can I add value to this individual and serve them as their new leader?* This is a question I keep at the forefront of my mind throughout my time working with that specific member of our team.

As I moved past that initial experience of being the proverbial "bull in a china shop" leader, I have recognized increasingly over time the importance of quieting your ego and not overtrying to prove your importance to your team. It eventually dawned on me that when I chose to behave this way, I was not proving myself to the people I was trying to impress in the first place, but rather working to prove myself to me. Re-channeling that effort and energy externally to deeply understand those I have the opportunity to serve as a leader has been much more rewarding and fruitful. As an example, five years ago when I became the new Vice President of Sales, I took over a senior sales team where the entire team was both older than I was and had been in the industry much longer than I had been. Moving from being a former peer to their leader, it could have been easy to fall back into the trap of working to impress versus serve. Luckily, I had the earlier "teaching moment" to draw upon and not make that same mistake.

This "team member first" approach was reinforced for me recently when I had the opportunity to connect with one of my former direct reports. We sat down together and caught up, and she articulated how much my personal approach to leadership meant to her. There was a specific time period, which she called out during our conversation, that was incredibly trying for her as a person. She expressed significant gratitude for our relationship and my supportive approach during this time as her leader. I was honored by her words and fulfilled because she felt led and cared for as a person versus an employee.

Caring about the people you lead isn't something that can be faked. During my playing days, Coach Hironaka showed genuine care with small, simple acts that showed all of his players what they meant to him. In fact, he never stopped with these simple acts. Each year on my birthday, Thanksgiving, and Christmas I still receive a personal text message or phone call from him, wishing me and my family well. He still does this for all his former players—that's hundreds of players over a 30+ year career. My hope and objective are that my effort, in serving those I have the opportunity to lead, has a similar impact on them as Coach Hironaka's approach had on me.

## NOT LISTENING

Joe Terry, President, Aptology

**It** was a beautiful day on the Big Island. Hot, but that's expected. Relatively still water and not a lot of wind, which were not expected, but a nice and welcome surprise. Great conditions for a personal record (PR) in the Ironman World Championships in Kona.

Due in part to the great conditions and some extra focus in my training, the swim went well and after the transition, I was in a good place. Fifty miles into the 112-mile bike leg and I was feeling really good. My inclination was to push harder, "pedal to the metal," as they say. Maybe, just maybe, I began to think, I could not only beat my personal best but blow it away.

But soon I heard my coach's words in my ear: "Slow down and eat." But I fought those words, thinking, *I am feeling so good, and I'm really not that hungry*. I was inclined not to follow his guidance. But I heard his voice again. *Slow down*. He said it again with greater intensity. I knew he was right. There was still a long way to go and many great obstacles ahead, namely the headwinds of the Queen K and a marathon in the blistering hot sun of Kona. If I didn't slow down, conserve my energy, and get the fuel I needed, this would get ugly. This was "not a sprint," as they say. Although my gut told me different, I acquiesced. It turned out to be the right decision. I had the energy I needed to get through the headwind on the back half of the bike ride and the strength I needed to endure the intense heat during the 26.2-mile run. I didn't crash and burn, and I did get that Kona PR I was seeking once the long day was over.

I wish I could say I always slow down when I need to and listen as well as I should, but I don't.

Both in racing and in my roles leading organizations, I like to go fast. I have a lot of confidence in my gut decisions; the little voice in my mind always tells me to trust my gut, make decisions fast, and not waste time. But that's not always the right choice.

In fact, slowing down and listening to the people on my team and across the organization has almost always led to better decisions. My people were close to the action, and sometimes closer to the business and to our customers, and therefore saw things I didn't. I've learned over time that people need to weigh in before they buy in. "Seeking first to understand," as Stephen Covey says, is important, especially when talking about the most important things and making big decisions in your organization.

When I resisted my tendency to make decisions alone in order to go fast, I have found that our company benefited. When our leaders were involved in the decision-making process, not only were decisions better but including my team ensured that they feel appreciated and respected, which led to greater commitment on their part.

Distancing yourself from the competition in an individual sport is good, but distancing yourself from the people in your organization is not so good for organizations that are trying to win—and win *together*.

---

## BEING TOO INVOLVED

G. Shawn Hunter, CEO, Mindscaling,
author of *Small Acts of Leadership*

**It** was 2006. Mariah Carey and Beyoncé topped the charts, the movie *Borat* was released, Google purchased YouTube for $1.6 billion, Pluto's planet status was revoked, Nintendo released the Wii, and Italy won the World Cup.

At this same moment in time, our mighty little company Targeted Learning was gaining speed and momentum. We were creating on-demand and live video learning content. Somehow, miraculously, we were ahead of the market. Just a few years earlier we were defining the market, and now competition was rising swiftly and steadily. I remember at one company off-site retreat, we had identified a handful of companies entering our space. The following year we lost count.

We were big enough to have people dedicated to sales, marketing, operations, technology, service, partnerships, and more. Yet we were also small enough that the 20 of us could still keep in close touch. And during this time, I had my hands in everything.

I was working with our technology team to design and build our next generation user experience, I was creating the content and product we sold, and I was leading or participating in almost all sales initiatives. I remember at one point, we had a fabulous sales guy who created a chart depicting who worked on what in the company—kind of like a Venn diagram showing who works where. My name was everywhere. I felt personally responsible for everything.

And I was stressed. I didn't realize or understand how stressed I was until we sold the company in early 2007, and I collapsed for a few months in an exhausted fog. The problem—my mistake—was that I was having a hard time letting go. I was having a hard time placing trust in my colleagues. What I have come to believe now is that I couldn't let go of a personal sense of ownership and responsibility, and felt I had to add my comments or approval to every strategy, every project, every decision. Upon reflection, I can now see I was lacking appropriate humility and over-valuing my importance to our work. I wasn't trusting the contributions of others, and the fundamental cause was that I didn't yet possess a strong sense of gratitude for their work. After all, if I have my hands in everything and I'm the principal reason for the success, why develop a sense of gratitude for someone else's contribution?

Once we sold the company to Skillsoft, and we entered the much larger corporation as a small division and product line, it was no longer possible for me to contribute everywhere, although initially I did try. I would ask to sit in on contract meetings and intellectual property discussions, and review marketing copy. After a while it was clear I was diluting my efforts, and I wasn't making meaningful contributions.

For me, the key was to learn and practice a deepened sense of gratitude for others, which in turn allowed me to give trust and let go. Targeted Learning was handicapped by my insistence to participate in (maybe even control) everything, but once we entered the much bigger world of Skillsoft, it became impossible, and I learned to be grateful for my colleagues and their skills and contributions.

As I traveled the world working with team members within Skillsoft, I began to actively let each collaborator know how grateful I was—grateful for the invitation to be helpful, grateful for learning from them, grateful for the opportunity to work with their clients. Eventually, this practiced and learned sense of gratitude allowed me to let go of what I could not control and instead focus on my real expertise.

The need to be overly involved in every aspect of the organization disappeared. I felt relief at the reduced pressure from what I couldn't, and didn't need to control, and the people in my organization felt more empowered, respected, and appreciated for their great contributions.

I have an expression I use in my writing: "Only do what only you can do." By following this guidance, I know my work is more valuable to others, and my impact as a leader is deeper and stronger.

## NOT EXPRESSING GRATITUDE

Dave Kroll, Vice President,
Global Communications, Qlik

**Sunday,** July 10, 1994 was a beautiful, sunny day for baseball at Candlestick Park in San Francisco. With rumors of a baseball strike in the weeks ahead, fans showed up in droves to watch the Giants play the Phillies in the last game before the all-star break. Although the fans came to watch their team, they also got to witness the "breakout" performance of the South Bay musical acoustic duo, not-so-cleverly named *Dave and Mike.* I was the Dave.

Despite our not-so-massive following in the South Bay, we had submitted our demo tape to the Giants the year prior, and with luck, a cancellation came with short notice just days before that game. The call went out to Dave and Mike to sing the national anthem.

Anxious and exhilarated, we sang our two-part harmony version of the anthem for the largest crowd we had or would ever perform in front of—and as we wrapped up, all 48,263 fans gave us a standing ovation and gave us shout-outs or high-fives when they saw us in the stands for the rest of the ballgame. I understood their recognition was more for the song than for us, but it still felt pretty darn good. Applause, along with tips in the tip jar when we played our three-hour sets at much smaller venues were the only form of gratitude Mike and I received for our music. They were simple gestures by our audiences that were always much appreciated and inspired us to play and sing our hearts out.

When I started working in technology firms in Silicon Valley, the gratitude was much harder to come by. In the analytical, fast-paced world of high tech, critiques of my work were much more plentiful than the "*attaboys.*" As a young professional in the communications industry, I remember the draft of my first press release marked up with what felt like dozens upon dozens of mistakes and corrections highlighted in a bright red marker, affectionately left on my desk chair by my supervisor. *Nice.* I remember another time I sent a company-wide email to about 30 people and shortly thereafter received a reply-all back from our CEO, with redline edits and grammar corrections as an example for all of us to learn from. *Ouch.* Both instances were painful and embarrassing, especially since my mom was an English teacher—sorry, Jane! But these were not exceptions; I'd often go weeks at a time between compliments, but rarely did a day go by without comments or criticisms at work by my supervisors, intended to improve my performance.

When I was promoted into my first management job, I followed the example I had been taught by my previous leaders. I thought my job was to make my employees better by focusing on correcting their flaws and mistakes to improve them. So, I seldom gave praise and often gave critical and negative feedback on a regular basis. Like a parent focusing on the one B+ rather than the six A's on a report card, my people felt underappreciated, and I'm sure, at times, demoralized. This was a costly error I made as a young leader and contributed to some truly great people leaving my team and company for other opportunities. The loss of those key people—at least in part due to my mistakes—really stung and was something that stayed with me and shook me up a bit, motiving me to look for better ways to improve my leadership abilities.

I read books about leadership and sought advice from leaders I respected. Addressing my mistakes head-on, I tried experimenting with different forms of recognition and more frequent "on the spot" compliments to acknowledge good work. It's amazing how a "thank you" helps people feel appreciated. In addition, I arranged more team dinners after long projects that had required extra-long hours and sacrifice by the team. For several teams, I printed up team dog tags to improve team cohesion as we went through challenges together, and I gave out medals for stand-out performances. Other actions included awarding small bonuses with cash for great efforts or delivering a bottle of wine to a teammate for doing something *right*. I think the team appreciated the authentic effort and intent behind it, and the size of the gift or bonus didn't really matter. I even got "the Mike" into the act on occasion to sing happy birthday in two-part harmony over the phone to employees on their special day. A bit unorthodox, but it achieved the goal of showing appreciation and recognizing employees—something I had not done naturally.

I learned that in life and work, people appreciate the small things. And I realized an important insight . . . recognition is free! It's been well researched that people don't stay at a job for the money; they stay because of their boss, their team, an inspiring mission, and strong company culture. Many leaders are *way* too stingy, thinking that if they recognize or reward too many people, it will water down and reduce the value of that recognition. I've never been a part of a company or heard of one, ever, where people left because they recognized people too much. Try it and see what happens with your teams.

While a number of the companies *talk* about engagement and valuing their employees, I joined Rackspace in 2013 and knew I'd found a company that actually *lived* it. Graham Weston, the co-founder and former Rackspace CEO and Chairman, said this about work: "What we all want is to be valued members of a winning team on an inspiring mission."

Read that again. Isn't that true for most everyone? These were not just words. They were lived every day and reinforced in the actions by "Rackers" up, down, and across the organization. It's a unifying statement that guided employees on how to treat each other—and not just as teammates, but as human beings. It permeated processes like new employee orientation, how leaders managed their employees, and it helped create an environment I liked to call the "no a-hole factor," where inspiring leaders could flourish, and self-focused, egotistical, or harsh leaders would eventually leave the company due to "organ rejection."

There are so many other ways to make people feel valued: stepping out of their way, focusing on their strengths and allowing their great ideas to flourish, and being open and authentic with them. These behaviors can create a cohesive, motivated, and engaged team. In the end, for me, leadership is about aligning people's gifts and strengths with where the company is going and where their strengths are needed most. Focusing on people's strengths brings their passion alive in the workplace. And regular and authentic recognition is one of the cheapest and easiest ways not only to keep people motivated and inspired, but also to pull their best work and effort from them.

People are smart. And, in the end, I've learned so much more from the people I managed than I ever taught them. In many ways, learning to express gratitude was a key part of my growth as a leader.

Currently, as the VP of Global Communications at Qlik, I carry with me the same enthusiasm for appreciation, gratitude, and the small acts of leadership that help me navigate the day-to-day challenges of a high-tech business.

---

# LEADER SELF-ASSESSMENT

Please rate yourself as you believe your team members would rate you on the following skills and talents by choosing the appropriate number from the terms below. Then total the numbers to see your overall self-assessment for this category.

| LOUSY | NEEDING TO IMPROVE | OK | PRETTY GOOD | OUTSTANDING |
|---|---|---|---|---|
| 1 | 2 | 3 | 4 | 5 |

**Do I fail to connect with my team?**

_______ 1. My team would say I am __________ at being open and vulnerable.

_______ 2. My team would say I am __________ at getting to know the members of the team.

_______ 3. My team would say I am __________ at listening.

_______ 4. My team would say I am __________ at giving them the right amount of guidance and support (not too much and not too little) for the team to succeed.

_______ 5. My team would say I am __________ at expressing gratitude.

________ **Connection total**

---

23+ = Outstanding—this is a real strength for you
18–22 = Pretty good—you are on your way to greatness
13–17 = OK—not bad (but do you really want to be an average leader?)
8–12 = Needing to improve—you have some work to do
5–7 = Lousy—this is a real challenge for you and therefore, for your team

# MISTAKE #3

## RUNNING TRULY AWFUL MEETINGS

YESTERDAY, IN OUR FOUR–HOUR MEETING, WE AGREED TO POST–PONE THE VENDOR SELECTION.
NO, WE AGREED TO USE OUR EXISTING VENDOR.
I THOUGHT WE AGREED TO CANCEL THE WHOLE PROJECT.
WE MIGHT NEED SOME CLARITY ON THIS.
FOUR MORE HOURS SHOULD DO IT.
Dilbert.com DilbertCartoonist@gmail.com
6-20-15 © 2015 Scott Adams, Inc. /Dist. by Universal Uclick

# RUNNING TRULY AWFUL MEETINGS

Several years ago, I was hired as the VP of Western U.S. and Canada for a technology company headquartered on the East Coast of the United States. I flew back to the company headquarters for my first executive team meeting, excited about meeting the colleagues I hadn't yet met, and working together with my new peers on the most important things facing our company.

The meeting was a two-day meeting, and in the first few hours, the team covered the following topics:

- Key accounts
- Customer support issues and churn
- Business unit status reports
- The right coffee for the break room
- Employee performance issues
- Implementing Sarbanes-Oxley compliance regulations
- Repaving the headquarters parking lot
- New HR benefits options
- A new product version release
- A potential future meeting (a meeting *about* meetings!)
- The new employee smartphone policy
- A potential acquisition

It was a smorgasbord of topics: administrative, strategic, tactical, some important to the business and this executive team, and many, probably most, clearly not worthy of our time.

On the cover of Patrick Lencioni's book *Death by Meeting*, there is a picture of an employee at the end of the conference table with his head down, either asleep or bored to tears. Not only does the title say a lot about deadly meetings, but the picture adds salt to the wound. Everyone in my executive meeting that day, who was not presenting at that moment, felt like that cover guy. As leaders, if we are honest with ourselves, we've all probably led that very meeting at some point over the course of our career. In the book, Patrick presents a very specific meeting model that has been vetted with thousands of executive teams over the years. He makes the case that there should be different types of meetings for different specific purposes and that by mixing the purposes and random topics for each, you end up with "meeting stew," which never tastes good. And in this meeting, the various chefs were making the biggest pot of this stew I'd ever tasted, and every bite was predictably hard to swallow.

Eyes glazed over and unanimous boredom set in as leaders took turns presenting slide after slide after slide. The agenda meandered aimlessly from item to item without closure to any of the items discussed, and I began to question my decision to take this position and join this company.

As my mind wandered, a peer of mine, sitting next to me, gave me a look that said he wanted my attention. He was my sales leadership counterpart with responsibility for the eastern U.S., and he was taking out a piece of scratch paper and looking at me as if to say, "This note is for you." I became interested and silently guessed at what the note might say.

Maybe he was writing out a short "welcome to the company" and offering support as I worked to become acclimated. Or perhaps there was an account with presence in both of our geographies that he wanted to strategize on and work together. Knowing that he previously had worked with many people across the company, maybe he was going to give insight on some of the leaders or employees on my team that he knew well to help me as I established myself with my team. I highly anticipated his note, whatever it said, because I knew it had to be more interesting than the multiple random topics and blather that was this meeting.

He handed the short note to me and as I opened it, there were only three words: Kill, Me, and Now. Kill Me Now!

I knew this leader was going to be a great friend of mine in the company because that's exactly what I was thinking. Kill me now! But the reality was that almost everyone in the room was thinking the same thing. There was absolutely no clarity as to the purpose of the meeting or what we were trying to accomplish. And in the instances where we did make some progress on a topic or decision, there was no confirmation of that decision nor the team's commitment to that decision. And at no time during that meeting did we end a conversation with clarity about what was decided and what we would communicate.

A leader I respect, Roy Aggarwal, serves as the chief of staff for the communications group in a large technology company. Roy is extremely passionate about good meetings and having lived in Asia as an ex-pat, he learned something about meetings while there that he applies to his business. I have heard him quote a Japanese saying, which loosely translated means "No target, no meeting." If there is no clarity about the meeting purpose, the meeting doesn't happen.

But let's face it. Meetings play an important role in organizations and can be a strategic tool if managed correctly. The trick is to make sure they are focused, held with appropriate purpose, and don't waste valuable time. In the pages that follow, five great leaders not only share their mistakes in this regard but offer their advice on how to avoid those mistakes to improve your business.

## ALLOWING CONFUSION ABOUT MEETINGS

Linda Copple Trout, Chief Justice,
Idaho Supreme Court (retired)

I served on the Idaho Supreme Court as a Justice for 15 years, seven as Chief and eight as an Associate Justice on the high court. In that time, I sat on over 1,800 cases and, of those, authored more than 400.

In a court of law, there is great clarity about a number of things. There is clarity about who is leading the case: the judge. It's clear what will be discussed and decided in each case, and specific rules and known, acceptable behaviors are followed to make sure order is kept and ensure justice is served. Protocols allow for appropriate debate, and procedures are followed as decisions are being made. And once made, there is not only understanding about what the decisions are but documentation of those decisions to ensure clarity. The inner workings of the courtroom are clear to everyone involved.

When I left the bench and took over as the Administrative Director of the Courts, though, I learned quickly that clarity was far less prevalent in other areas of the organization, especially in meetings. Often, our meetings lacked clarity of purpose, were uneven in participation, had no clear process, and decisions were often unrecorded or not communicated. And my sense, having talked to business and community leaders, was that this problem was pervasive across many organizations outside of the Courts and other government entities.

Not only did I recognize this across the organization, but it also became clear that my own executive leadership team staff meetings—for which I was responsible—also lacked clarity. And that's a big mistake. In any organization, employees watch the executive team very closely. That goes for all behaviors, including how meetings are run. If the leadership runs poor meetings, it cascades down and perpetuates itself.

After recognizing the challenge with meetings facing the Courts organization, I took steps to correct the problem. I talked to the Idaho Courts' Chief Information Officer who introduced me to a consultant. This person had helped him align his team and acquainted our team with a good, proven process for running effective, productive meetings. After some work together, the Idaho Courts' leadership team and I agreed on a new approach to our meetings: We would not only agree on appropriate behaviors for the meeting, but the meeting leader also would ensure we started and ended with clarity. We were clear up front about why we were there, and we were clear when we finished as to what had been decided, what the next steps were, and how we would communicate. With discipline in applying the process, our meetings became more productive, our leadership team became better aligned, and we set the tone for meetings across the organization.

Because I was both the first female justice and later the first female chief, early on in those roles I was worried about making mistakes lest they cause problems for future generations of women seeking a similar seat. But worse than making mistakes would be to learn nothing from them. Taking quick, decisive action after appropriate consideration worked for the Idaho Courts and worked elsewhere across the organization—and that included changing poorly run meetings to those that were productive and clear.

## FAILING TO START MEETINGS WITH CLARITY

Scott Ault, Executive Vice President,
Workplace Solutions, Mutual of Omaha

**If** there is one thing that drives me crazy as the leader of a large organization, it is unproductive or unnecessary meetings. Having talked to executive peers and leaders in other industries and companies, I know I am not alone in this.

I started my career in the insurance industry as a sales rep and have spent most of my career in jobs that have clear, direct sales quotas. These jobs have always come with great rewards if the quotas are achieved and a corresponding opportunity to "pursue other job options elsewhere" if they are not. Because of that intense focus on the goals and the ramifications for failure, I tried hard to avoid unproductive meetings that didn't get me closer to my goals. Likewise, as a sales manager, and later as a Director and Vice President of Sales, the focus was similarly clear. I coached my sales teams always to keep their eye on the prize, eliminate distractions, and make sure every action is in some way moving the ball down the field toward the goal line.

As I moved into more senior positions, I started having more and more time at the "home" office, and my days started to fill with meetings and requests for my time that were not necessarily aligned to our most important goals. Then, when I took my current position, leading the largest organization I have ever been responsible for, I realized this was true for the meetings *I* was responsible for: the meetings of *my* executive team. How did this happen?

I think I know the answer. Working in a sales organization is a lot like playing on a golf team. Golfers each have their individual scores, are clear on what they are trying to achieve individually, and at the end of the match you add up the scores to see who won. On a football team, on the other hand, players are interdependent, and different players in different positions must work together to achieve the goal of winning a game and ultimately a championship. While different in dependence and the teamwork required to win, both types of teams are absolutely clear about their goals.

I went from leading a golf team (running a sales organization), to now leading a football team (an organization with many different functions), and eventually saw that the goals of this kind of team were unclear in my new organization. I suspected that was why our meetings were not as productive and useful as they needed to be. Like a football team, we needed an overall goal that would be socialized across the organization. My mistake was not identifying that goal for the organization and making sure everyone knew it and was aligned around it.

Once my team and I realized this and worked together to create our number one priority, our thematic goal, we built a meeting structure and cadence that would align to it. It included different types of meetings for different purposes, as outlined in Patrick Lencioni's book *Death by Meeting*. Meeting types included: check-in meetings, weekly staff meetings, ad-hoc meetings, and quarterly meetings.

My team and I also created additional meetings to communicate and reinforce the newly created thematic goal across our business, adding monthly meetings for leaders across the enterprise and "all hands" meetings for the organization to make sure everyone both understood and felt ownership for that most important organizational goal. That may seem like a lot of meetings, but if they are aligned to the achievement of your most important goal, they are absolutely worth it.

The success we have had in our organization since we implemented this highly aligned meeting approach has proven that to be true.

Since the primary goal is communicated and socialized across the organization, all meetings are evaluated by their value with respect to our primary goal. Meetings not aligned are questioned and, in many cases, canceled, thus returning valuable time—the one resource that can't be replaced. With this kind of clarity, individual meeting requests or appointments also are more easily evaluated and denied if they fail the "alignment" test. While we value open communication and time spent with people in and out of our organization, that could be done in many ways other than one-on-one appointments. I began encouraging my leaders to take that same approach, telling them I'd rather have a healthy, successful, and aligned organization with people mad at us for not taking one-on-one meetings than to have an unhealthy, unsuccessful organization where we hold all meetings that are requested.

Clarity on our most important goal has helped us reduce the number of (crazy-making) unnecessary and unproductive meetings in our organization. I highly recommend the development of a top priority and a meeting structure aligned to it for any leaders who have similar challenges.

# FAILING TO ALLOW PRODUCTIVE CONFLICT

Steve Long, Global Vice President, Sales and Marketing, Intel, Client Computing Group

I am Latin. Although I was born in the United States, I have made my home in two countries in Latin America and have worked, traveled, and spent significant time in most of the others. At the risk of stereotyping a whole region, my experience is that many who live in that broad, diverse region are passionate and enjoy a good argument with friendly confrontation. I am no exception. I love to "mix it up"—to challenge ideas and debate opinions. I enjoy a good disagreement and embrace good constructive conflict. That is true at home and at work—and is definitely at its peak during the World Cup, which is distracting me as I write this.

A second thing that is true about me is that I have an extremely strong bias for action. I like to make decisions quickly, and once they are made I like to go full speed, implementing that decision with pace and urgency—knowing we may have to correct course along the way.

With these two things in mind, along with the well-known Intel mantra *disagree and commit*, it's no wonder that I have found a professional home at Intel and have stayed here for 18 years.

If you have worked with or for Intel any time during the past half century, you have probably heard the phrase *disagree and commit* many times. Coined first by Andy Grove, an Intel founder, long-time CEO, and true icon in the technology world, it is a mantra repeated and practiced daily throughout the Intel enterprise. The outcomes of this phrase and its practice have had a great impact on Intel's success since it was founded over 50 years ago.

The concept encourages disagreement and good productive conflict prior to a decision being made. But once that decision has been made, regardless of people's opinions and positions prior to the decision, everybody must commit to it and leave the meeting or conversation aligned. It helps leaders and teams avoid the consensus trap, where the lack of consensus could lead to inaction. Following that mantra also makes sure everyone is able to weigh in on an effort to make the best decision possible.

An important component to this principle is that the "disagree" must come *before* the "commit," and therein was my mistake.

Although I had been using the phrase and practicing this approach with teams since I started with Intel in 2000, I failed to deploy it when I took on my first executive leadership position at the company. I was hired as VP and GM for Intel Latin America in late 2010 to drive results. To do that, I decided the region needed a simplified strategy. Notice I said *I* decided. I had inherited a large team that was, in most cases, older and more experienced than I was. Many had previously been my peers, some had been *my* senior leaders, years before, yet they were now all reporting to me as members of my staff.

The problem was not with the strategy I had inherited. The team had spent considerable time on it, and it was a good, solid strategy but was presented in a complex way. The problem was with rallying, communicating, and conquering the hearts of the broader sales team. To solve that problem, I focused on simplifying the strategy and tactics, and then framing it simply with key numbers 9-3-1: $9B in revenue; 3 key strategies to get us there; 1 unified team. When my staff eventually bought in, it helped focus and pave the way to achieve our key business metrics. The buy-in took longer than it needed to, however, because I failed to solicit my new leaders' opinions and ideas before moving forward.

Looking back, it seemed so obvious. But why didn't I follow proper *disagree and commit* protocol at the time?

Maybe I wanted to make a statement and demonstrate my authority as the new *jefe* (boss) in charge, especially given past reporting relationships? Could it have been that I was concerned the leadership team would have been too enamored with the complexity of the prior approach and would be resistant to even wanting to change? Or maybe it was my own over-developed bias for wanting immediate action? Perhaps I was trying to save the expenses of flying in 15 leaders from across Latin America for one meeting, when we were set to get together at the sales kickoff in just a few weeks in the future?

More than likely it was a combination of all of these, paired with the fact that there was limited time before our sales kickoff, and I wanted a plan. The important point here is that I did not ask for the team's input, nor did I honor their wealth of experience as I should have. I pulled the content together and presented it to the organization in our sales kick-off without getting the senior leaders' full buy-in. While the broad organization rallied—there was no chance for the leadership team to disagree—as you might expect, mixed commitment followed.

I can only imagine the colorful names I was called in a variety of languages, probably deservedly so, by my new team within that first month of my new job!

Bottom line? I blew it. I had to unwind—take a step back—and recoil before moving forward. Only when I admitted the mistake with the direct team and allowed the debate to happen, did the leadership team make great strides toward a commitment to achieve the 9-3-1 plan.

I then took on a new role in the organization as the Global VP of Sales and Marketing for the Intel Client Computing Group (CCG). My organization and goals are much larger and my team even more diverse. Having learned from the above mistake, I try hard now to slow down to allow productive debate and to practice real *disagree and commit* protocol whenever a big decision must be made. This is even more important with a truly international team, spanning five continents and representing different cultures with different comfort levels with respect to conflict and debate—I've learned that I must be sensitive to these differences as I lead my organization.

My hope is that the 200 leaders in my organization will not follow my lead and repeat the mistake I made with my new team in Latin America eight years ago. If they allow for disagreeing *then* committing as they and their teams make important decisions for the good of the organization, I am confident the success we have enjoyed at Intel CCG will continue for at least the next 50 years.

---

## FAILING TO CLARIFY DECISIONS AND ACTIONS

Richard Brilliant, Chief Audit Officer and Senior Vice President, Risk Advisory and Assurance Services, Carnival Corporation

**Every** day, on the bridge of every one of the 100 ships in our fleet across all 10 Carnival Corporation cruise line brands, the ship engineers practice closed-loop communication.

"Five degrees to port." (Navigator)

"Five degrees to port." (Helmsman, repeats)

"Yes." (Navigator)

Closed-loop communication is a simple but effective communication technique used to avoid misunderstandings. When the sender gives a message, the receiver repeats it back verbatim. The sender then confirms the message by using the word "yes" or "confirmed." If the receiver incorrectly repeats the message, the sender will say "negative" and then repeat the process until there is no ambiguity. Only then are appropriate actions taken.

Clarity of communication on the bridge is paramount, a non-negotiable for the officers and seamen navigating our ships. The safety of our passengers and our crew depends upon it. Likewise, clarity is paramount when the captain of each of our ships leads his daily meeting with his team of officers. This is critical in that the captain and all of his staff have different challenges and different problems they are facing every day.

The captain's top priorities—what keeps him or her up at night—are safety and schedule. Keeping the passengers and crew safe is first and foremost, but keeping to the schedule, getting our vessel where it needs to be on time, is another high priority. Not only is the failure to stay on schedule a customer service issue, but there are significant costs associated with being late into or out of port.

The cruise director's top priority, on the other hand, has always been making sure our guests are having fun and are entertained. And how does one have fun on one of our ships? Eating, drinking, gaming, dancing, education events, beauty treatments, and fitness classes are just a few of the many ways our guests enjoy themselves while on board. The responsibilities and daily priorities of those two key officers, as well as the others in that meeting, could be very different at times. It is critical that before their daily meeting is over, they leave with perfect alignment about decisions and actions.

I'd like to report that over the course of my career as a leader I have always ended meetings with absolute clarity about decisions and actions, but that wouldn't be true.

Early in my career, I was promoted to my first significant leadership role, moving from an individual contributor role to a Manager of Audit Services. As I know can be true in many cases, I was promoted due to my functional area skill and expertise, not my experience leading people, and certainly not because I ran great meetings. The meetings I ran as a new leader, having had no training, little guidance, and few great meeting role models, were not only boring and lacked focus, but often ended with confusion. This led to misunderstandings between members of my staff, mistakes—therefore extra work in audits done by my team—and delays in getting audits completed. And, as you might expect, my internal customer relationships suffered, and levels of engagement and morale for the people I was leading were lower than they could have been.

I've learned over time that a key leadership responsibility is to force clarity, especially with respect to roles, appropriate behaviors, communications, and decisions made in meetings. As my responsibilities have grown, the risks associated with a lack of clarity have grown dramatically as well. Mistakes due to confusion on the part of the organization that I now lead, Risk Advisory and Assurance Services, can lead to safety issues, regulatory and compliance problems, and significant fines for the organization, all of which are unacceptable.

We simply can't put our guests or employees in jeopardy because we communicated poorly.

One simple meeting protocol we follow religiously to ensure excellence in communication is simple, but especially effective. We save the last five minutes of every staff meeting to re-state the decisions and actions, and note who is responsible for each. Although it may sound simple and obvious, my experience is that more often than not, this last step is needed to clarify a key point or assignment decision. That simple practice allows for greater alignment of my leadership team as we disembark for our next meeting and ensure better alignment across my department.

I'll close the loop on this with one final communication in hopes of avoiding confusion:

"As a leader, we should always end our meetings with clarity."

"As a leader, we should always end our meetings with clarity."

"Yes."

## LEAVING MEETINGS WITHOUT CLEAR MESSAGING

Marc Cameron, Managing Director,
Rio Tinto Kennecott Copper

**Safety.** It has always been our most important focus at Rio Tinto Kennecott Copper, and it is embedded in everything we do. It's not only our first core value and number one priority, but it is an important component in all of our key strategies and decisions.

We track safety incidents very closely, and when an incident occurs, we take it personally as a leadership team and across the organization. Although we strive to avoid all incidents completely, in a business like ours, 100 percent success at all times is an especially challenging aspiration. When incidents do occur, we spend a lot of time deconstructing what went wrong—what we might've done better—to ensure we avoid similar incidents in the future.

If you don't care about safety and are not willing to commit to continuous improvement and focus in this area, you're not going be happy working at Rio Tinto. And, truth be told, if you don't care about safety, we don't want you here.

Across the Rio Tinto enterprise, and specifically here at Kennecott Copper, we start every meeting with a "zero harm" share about health and safety so that it is top of mind right from the start. And, while the safety focus is absolutely critical, we also have to have clarity about the other business issues we will be discussing so that upon leaving the meeting, we are able to ensure the organization is aligned and informed with respect to our plans and decisions.

As a professional engineer, my functional area of expertise has been marked by precision, design, logic, and great attention to detail. This is what engineers do best. What we generally are not known for, however, is our outstanding communication skills—and I am no exception. Communicating effectively and repeatedly has always been an area of continuous personal improvement. But in my role with Kennecott Copper, with the safety of over 2,000 employees and contractors in jeopardy, there is no place for a communication breakdown. The impact on our people and their family, friends, and loved ones due to a significant incident is at stake, and there is no room for me to communicate poorly.

Recognizing my personal challenges in this area, I discussed the issue with my executive team and we agreed we could all do better. We needed to improve as a team and put a process in place to make sure to leave our meetings knowing what we decided and what we would be communicating as *one voice* with our extended teams. We brought in an expert in this area who presented a proven model and structure for better meetings, which required ending with clarity and cascading messages, but I also dug deep into my personal experience for a technique to fine tune the approach.

I recalled something I learned while playing and coaching hockey: The best hockey coaches were always willing to stop play right in the middle of practice to ensure the agreed-upon practice plan was being executed correctly. In fact, the best coaches had no problem stopping play multiple times to ensure the team knew exactly what was supposed to be happening at every moment on the ice. Stopping to point out a play that was run well was a great way to reinforce the behavior and increase skill and the likelihood of success. Likewise, stopping play in a practice when things went poorly had an equally powerful instructive effect. Clearly communicating what went wrong and what could be improved kept the team and players from making the same error again. When direction was given and repeated, there was no mistake about who should be doing what, out on the ice. Over-communication brought clarity, helped get the most out of our limited ice time at our practices, and ultimately helped us win more games.

As my executive team implemented our new meeting structure and cadence, I decided to deploy this same strategy. With many important things to discuss, our weekly meetings were often long, and it was easy to lose track of decisions and commitments if there wasn't this consistent, deliberate focus. I decided I would stop every meeting three specific times to summarize and reconfirm the decisions and actions made. And three is just the minimum. The team and I agreed anyone can stop the meeting to check commitments and corresponding messages as often as necessary, in order to improve communication during and, importantly, after our meetings. The results have been dramatic.

Since deploying these measures and being more deliberate about our messaging, we have received a lot of great qualitative feedback about the better and clearer messages coming out of our team meetings. The engineer in me loves data and metrics, though, and I am happy to report that since being so focused on communication, many of the key business metrics we watch carefully—including employee engagement levels and Net Promoter Scores—are up significantly. And, most importantly, our metrics regarding our top priority, safety, improved at the same time, with the number of incidents and corresponding absentee rates dropping to near-historic lows.

The mining business is not a game. But I am grateful for the lessons I learned from my past coaches about how best to communicate and win in our business.

---

# LEADER SELF-ASSESSMENT

Please rate yourself as you believe your team members would rate you on the following skills and talents by choosing the appropriate number from the terms below. Then total the numbers to see your overall self-assessment for this category.

| LOUSY | NEEDING TO IMPROVE | OK | PRETTY GOOD | OUTSTANDING |
|---|---|---|---|---|
| 1 | 2 | 3 | 4 | 5 |

**Do I run truly awful meetings?**

_______ 1. My team would say I am __________ at ensuring clarity about our meetings.

_______ 2. My team would say I am __________ at starting meetings with clarity.

_______ 3. My team would say I am __________ at allowing for productive conflict in our meetings.

_______ 4. My team would say I am __________ at ensuring clarity of decisions, commitments, and actions during meetings.

_______ 5. My team would say I am __________ at ensuring we leave meetings with clear messaging.

_______ **Meetings total**

---

23+ = Outstanding—this is a real strength for you
18–22 = Pretty good—you are on your way to greatness
13–17 = OK—not bad (but do you really want to be an average leader?)
8–12 = Needing to improve—you have some work to do
5–7 = Lousy—this is a real challenge for you and therefore, for your team

# MISTAKE #4

## HIRING TOO FAST, FIRING TOO SLOW

ALICE, I WANT YOU TO INTERVIEW A JOB CANDIDATE. LET ME KNOW WHAT YOU THINK.
scottadams@aol.com
www.dilbert.com
WHY DID YOU LEAVE YOUR LAST JOB?
I PUNCHED MY BOSS.
4-2-08 © 2008 Scott Adams, Inc./Dist. by UFS, Inc.
HE'S EXACTLY WHAT WE NEED.

# HIRING TOO FAST, FIRING TOO SLOW

"Darlin', I got a promotion!" I shouted as I walked in the door, having just returned from a business trip. "Let's go celebrate!"

At least I thought it was a promotion . . .

Prior to this "promotion" I had been working for my medium-sized software company as an executive leader responsible for sales and support across a large U.S. and international geography. I was on a business trip between sales calls one day when our company's CEO and COO called me out of the blue to see if I would take on an additional sales unit. In that conversation, they shared that our company needed growth. Hmmm. I had never known a for-profit company that didn't. This was especially important to our company in the year ahead, they said, and they were hoping I would build a new team of "hunters" to go after key accounts that had never done business with our organization before.

I'd have a sizeable training and education budget to work with, could hire a sales director to run that new unit, and would have the ability to hire as many as 10 new salespeople (and pay them extremely well) right out of the gate. They stroked my ego by noting that I had been especially strong at new business sales over time and, knowing my commitment and the passion I had for the company, "closed" me on the opportunity by reiterating how important it was to the company and its future. Flattering me by saying I was the exact guy they wanted for the important role worked—I said yes, right then and there on that call.

(A salesperson, if you don't already know, is the easiest person in the world to sell to, and this was a good instance of that scenario. My editor/wife reminds me as I write this that I agreed to the position, which promised both additional responsibility and a lot of additional work, without the promise of more money and with much greater risk than my current position.)

I hired a sales director I knew and trusted (I'll call her Beth), and we got to work building the hunting team. Knowing the historical ramp time for salespeople in our company and knowing also the length of our typical sales cycle, Beth and I had to move fast in building our team. And the regular calls from the CEO regarding the status of hiring, at least two in the first week after I took the position, added to the pressure to hire and hire fast.

You already know where this is going.

Beth and I had about 20 years of collective leadership experience between us, and we absolutely knew that we should hire with close attention to our corporate culture and fit. But we didn't. We knew that we should check references and a whole lot of them and really get to know these candidates, but we didn't do that either. And we knew that hiring super quickly when desperate was a bad idea, but in a tight labor market with a big bogey and limited time to achieve it, we did just that.

The results were predictable. Bad employees, poor results, and the intense, multiple, recurring headaches that the wrong employees invariably cause. The worst of the hires turned out to be professional sales job seekers, not workers, *seekers*—total scam artists—who faked their histories, set up phone numbers and fake business names, and acted as one another's key references while they took on multiple jobs and milked the companies for money until they were discovered. They preyed on leaders like us who were so desperate to hire that they cut corners on hiring, rushed the process, and ultimately got exactly what they deserved.

We didn't make our number that year (shocking!) and probably only saved our jobs with a big deal at the end of the year to make the numbers respectable. That deal was closed by an employee who had come over from another business unit, who had been hired the right way, with the right timing, and for the right reasons.

So embarrassing.

I don't know if there is any other type of leadership mistake that is so common and causes such a visceral reaction in leaders than the mistakes made with respect to hiring and firing. You show me an experienced leader without a story or two of hiring or firing poorly, and I will share with you the name I have for that leader: LIAR.

With so many examples of leaders who made mistakes around hiring and firing as I conducted my research, it was hard to choose the ones to highlight in the pages that follow. But the five leaders on the following pages not only have great stories about mistakes regarding hiring and firing, but have smart ideas on things to remember at both the front and back end of the employee life cycle.

## HIRING WITHOUT ALIGNMENT TO PURPOSE

Christine Talbot, Senior Vice President, Human Resources, World Vision, U.S.

At World Vision, we have always been very clear about who we are: "World Vision is a Christian humanitarian organization dedicated to working with children, families, and their communities worldwide to reach their full potential by tackling the causes of poverty and injustice . . ." It is front and center on our website, in all of our communications internally, and reiterated with partners and donors. And around the world, the vision is communicated and lived every day in the 100 countries where our employees and partners work to reach our goal: "Life in all its fullness for every child."

While I have been the senior executive of human resources, it has been my responsibility to see that we supported the organization's talent needs, spanning all phases of engagement through the full life cycle of a staff member. This included recruiting, hiring, onboarding, training, managing performance and benefits, and then retirement from the organization. Meeting the needs for talent is one of the most critical tasks of an organization, and getting it right on the front end in selection of talent is paramount—arguably the most important part of the talent equation. I learned this the hard way as an executive leader at a previous employer.

I was a senior leader at a major not-for-profit healthcare system and, as technology requirements and complexities grew exponentially, we needed to hire a number of senior technology leaders to fill a critical gap in our organization. The right candidates would need to have great technology expertise; strong experience managing large technical units in an organization as well as with many complex technical projects; and be adept at building an organization capable of meeting both our immediate technology needs and those in the future for the whole hospital system. As we interviewed multiple candidates, only a few stood out as meeting all of *those* criteria. But there was one criterion we didn't consider enough: The candidate needed to be aligned with our purpose. We hired these new executive leaders who could meet our immediate technology needs, but soon learned that they lacked passion for the mission of the organization, for our industry, and for patient care.

We recognized the misalignment relatively quickly after making the hires, but discovered as time went on that it was a larger mistake than we first knew. As senior leaders often do, our new leaders hired a lot of "their" people, most of whom were unfamiliar with the inner workings of not-for-profit companies. Seeking to be successful, they moved quickly to get results, often without pausing to gain an appreciation for the history, mission, and broader interest of the organization. These were smart people who were skilled and excited to participate in the building out of new technology.

But similar to the new leaders who hired them, they cared very little about the mission. And with no tie to the business and its purpose, only to the technology, they often left abruptly when exciting projects ended or when they were recruited to better paying opportunities elsewhere. The churn of leadership turnover, change, and constant adaptation resulted in uncertainty, chaos, jockeying for approval, and general distraction. The HR organization was pressed to support a leadership team divided by old and new, mission focused and individual success focused. The predictable result was expensive turnover and strained internal relationships across divisions. Charged with oversight of the hiring, these challenges and selection mismatches felt painful to me as a leader.

When I came to World Vision in early 2015, I was determined not to allow that same mistake. I was happy that the World Vision purpose was a critical part of my screening before I was hired. Rich Stearns, the CEO who would be my manager, interviewed me in the executive conference room where pictures of the poor with whom he had personally interacted lined the walls, each with a story he could tell. He shared some of those stories of hope and transformation. As a decade-long World Vision child sponsor, I was already "in" on the mission to some degree. My visit to the headquarters and that interview with Rich, including his tears as he spoke of those served by World Vision, cemented my desire to join the mission of serving the poor around the world.

While we focus on fit from a purpose and values standpoint for every hire, we are especially careful when we hire leaders. It's not that we value people differently—as a Christian organization we believe that every person is created in God's image and that we are all equal. But in a large organization, when you hire a leader—especially a senior leader who will be representing the company and hiring many employees—the impact of misaligned hiring can be exponential, and even more so when joining a mission-driven organization.

Our rigorous approach to hiring leaders includes three criteria that we use as filters in the process. Managers must have a servant leadership approach to their staff, as well as functional area competency. The right leaders must have a passion for our purpose, along with a willingness to dedicate their professional life to helping the poor, including an expectation and openness to the transformation of one's own understanding of God's heart for the poor. Typically, leaders hired from for-profit environments take a significant downshift from robust compensation packages in order to serve with us. And, finally, leaders must be aligned to our Christian values and be willing and able to integrate our shared faith into their leadership mindsets and behaviors, and consciously live out our core values.

We recently applied that same rigorous hiring process to our most important position of all: a new CEO to replace Rich Stearns, who had successfully and faithfully led our organization for 20 years. The Board of Directors, who was responsible for the hire, applied those same criteria to ensure fit, and the result was an outstanding hire for the future of our organization.

Although there were hundreds of impressive prospects and a resulting candidate slate, the final result was the hiring of Edgar Sandoval, a true servant leader who had lived our purpose and had demonstrated his commitment to it during his previous three years as World Vision's Chief Operating Officer. Having worked alongside him for these past few years, his fit for the position and alignment to our purpose were clear. I knew he would continue to live our purpose and demonstrate it across the organization and outside of the organization on a daily basis. And I was also certain that with his leadership we would work hard to see that every hire we made would allow us to help communities lift themselves out of poverty.

## HIRING WITHOUT ALIGNMENT TO VALUES

Duncan Richardson, Co-Founder and CEO,
Bodies in Motion

**My** wife, Rachel, and I are black belts in Taekwondo. So are all four of our kids, ages 15, 12, 10, and 8 at the time of this writing. I guess that's not too surprising given that Rachel and I are black belt master instructors and run a small business called Bodies in Motion, where we teach Taekwondo to hundreds of people each year. Regardless of their "unfair advantage" in achieving that designation, with us as parents, it took each of the four kids years of hard work, and we are super proud of them. As a family, some of the things that are important to us are having fun, being disciplined and fit, and caring for and about others. These values also align nicely to some of the core values of our business: "commitment to work," "commitment to guests," and "fun."

Rachel and I started The Academy of Taekwondo 17 years ago after graduating from Boise State University. She was a cheerleader, and I was the mascot, Buster Bronco, on the sidelines of all the Boise State Football games. Go Broncos! With our passion for the martial arts, exercise, and a shared preference for constant activity, we should have known that the more traditional, more sedentary jobs we took immediately after college would never be a fit. And, with that in mind, we started our own Taekwondo studio that, over time, became Bodies in Motion.

As our business gained traction and grew from the two of us to three and then four, on its way to the 37 employees we have today, we were having trouble hiring all *great* people. We took great care as owners to do well at hiring but, at the time, were at about a 60/40 split between *great* employees that we would *absolutely* rehire, and *good* employees that we would *probably* rehire. I suppose that's a mistake on its own, but my real mistake was not having a strong process to *know* if the candidates were an absolutely great fit. One thing we did know was that if we were going to grow our business to scale, we needed great people who aligned to our values and would delight our customers.

Having heard stories of great companies like Southwest Airlines, Nordstrom, and Zappos working hard to find the right candidates and taking clever approaches in their interviewing process, we developed our own creative approach. The purpose was to make sure anyone we hired, now or in the future, would align to the two most important and difficult values to discern in an interview: "commitment to guests" and "fun."

After some trial and error with the order of events and process, we found an approach that worked well. We start with a group interview (a group of applicants), although we don't go out of our way to make applicants aware of that as we schedule them in. This is the first of many fun surprises in our process for hiring for camp counselors as well as other team members.

As a group, the organizer encourages the applicants to introduce themselves to one another and then to ask each other questions during the approximate 20 minutes prior to the time when the actual interview would begin. What they don't realize is that the interview has already begun. Along with real candidates in this "get to know you" conversation are several "motioneers" (our employees), in disguise pretending to be candidates. They use this time to determine the applicants' ability to have fun, be kind, and treat people with respect. I never want to miss these interviews for many reasons, but the best one is the look on the candidates' faces when the leader of the process says, "Will all the motioneers in the group please step forward?" Priceless.

Part two of the group interview includes speed-dating questions with motioneers and the candidates moving around quickly to get to know one another. Creative questions like, "Tell me about your favorite book, but do it in a pirate voice," and other questions that discern their activity levels and the ways they make fun are also critical to this part of the interview.

Part three is a mock birthday party where two candidates at a time are instructed to stand in front of a birthday-party-sized group of candidates, and motioneers pretend to be birthday party guests, and perform an impromptu skit. The purpose is to see how they might make a spontaneous situation fun and show how they might entertain our guests—whether at a birthday party, working at the front desk, as a barista in our coffee shop, or as a fitness instructor. This interview process might sound awful to you—and if so, you need not apply!

Once these steps in the interview process are complete, we do more formal interviews with those who hadn't backed out or ones we hadn't otherwise disqualified. Even the formal interviews are designed to check for fun, commitment to guests, and also commitment to work. We screen finalists for these key qualities in other ways as well, such as asking for the references that *we* want, based upon their stories/histories and answers to questions, rather than the ones *they* might want to provide. Because this usually catches them off guard, we get a more accurate assessment of who they are as candidates.

Does your hiring process allow for clearly identifying candidates with the most important values to your business? I've found that if you discern what your most important and most difficult values are to hire for and find a way to aggressively and thoroughly screen for those, it can make a big difference. It will ensure all your employees are great ones, ones you would absolutely hire again, and will help you put your business in motion to achieve great things.

## HIRING WITHOUT ALIGNMENT TO CULTURAL FIT

Alex Potts, CEO, Loring Ward,
author of *The Wealth Solution*

**I've** heard it said that *culture trumps strategy*. In fact, the late Peter Drucker famously took it one step further saying, "Culture eats strategy for breakfast." Smart guy. I think we all can agree that a sound business strategy is critical if we want our organization to succeed. In fact, in my business I have relied on people who are much smarter than I am to help determine that strategy. But culture is a completely different issue. As CEO, I have to take responsibility for the culture and can't give that responsibility to anyone else. I consider myself not only the Chief *Executive* Officer, but the Chief *Culture* Officer as well. Culture is *that* important.

To establish a healthy culture, two things are critical: an aligned, example-led leadership team and clarity about what is most important to your business. Several years ago, I made a mistake on both of these fronts, and everyone involved suffered.

I had a key opening on my executive team, one that was going to be important to both the short-term key initiatives and the long-term success of the business. Unfortunately, I hadn't realized then what I now know: You need to identify and be clear about your core values *before* you hire a key executive. *Any* hire completed before you identify those values leaves success up to chance.

As we moved through the interview process for this key leader, one candidate stood out as the smartest, most strategic of the lot. He had worked at great companies and had done great things. His expertise and experience would surely help us overcome the challenges our business was facing. But there were small red flags my other leaders and I noticed that would have been glaring sirens (and disqualifiers, I am now certain) if we had previously identified our values and used them appropriately as a filter for these executive candidates.

We hired him. Almost immediately, my previously strong executive team began to weaken. Unexpected in-fighting led to issues in trust and confidence amongst peers. The newly born lack of trust on the executive team then started to cascade throughout the organization. Although the business was strong at that moment, I could see politics and confusion were becoming more prevalent and knew the strength of our business wouldn't last without regaining alignment on my team. Anyone could see that our team was in trouble and needed help getting back on track. I brought in a key adviser—someone I actually had known for more than 40 years—and we began dissecting the problem. Prior to those two days of working together as a team, the adviser shared with me some hard truths about my team and business. One of his especially poignant observations was that we would continue to have similar issues if we didn't set about the business of clarifying our values.

So, we got busy.

After two full days of hard work, one key outcome was that we had finally identified those core values. They are: "humble," "caring," and "smart-do." (Smart-do relates to a combination of intellectual and situational/people smarts and the willingness to figure things out to get things done: a can-do attitude.)

As part of that off-site event, we discussed that not only should these values be used to hire great people who would fit with our culture, these values should be used to move people out of the business who did not. We also discussed that if our executive team was not living and demonstrating those values daily, the new values would mean nothing to the organization and probably shouldn't even be shared with our extended teams. We finally had the clarity we needed on values and after the off-site, realized that this executive (who actually attended the off-site and helped define the core values!) was a poor choice and would have to leave the company. Ironically, the individual's lack of humility created a further issue as the individual thought they fully aligned with the core values!

Having applied those values as a filter across the whole executive team, it became apparent that there were actually *two* executive leaders on the team who were not a fit. If these were truly behaviors we absolutely wouldn't compromise on, they both would have to go.

Unfortunately, due to business realities and other extenuating circumstances, it took longer than it should have to move both of those executives off the team and out of the company. That's probably another mistake. Some of the increasing challenges and pain the company felt as the termination process took longer than ideal proved a great example of why hiring with alignment to core values is so critical.

Since the termination of those two leaders, we have made replacements to the executive team with two others who are humble, caring, and exhibit the smart-do attitude that we had determined is so important. The team is more cohesive, more trusting, the business is stronger, and the leaders and I talk about the importance of our core values with every opportunity. I can say the values now are fully steeped into our culture. The clear and concise values are our proverbial "North Star" and inform our hiring, successes, failures, and improvements within the business. Those values also serve to protect the most important component in our business: our culture.

---

## HIRING TOO FAST AND IGNORING RED FLAGS

Nick Schichtle, Vice President,
National Perm Practices, Adecco

**As** a young leader, still relatively new to the recruiting industry, I secured approval from the senior executives to hire two additional positions to take advantage of favorable market conditions. Our industry is a leading economic indicator, and this was one of those times when the market was especially strong. Unfortunately, that meant the demand for the subject matter experts I needed was high, while supply was low. I was thrilled to find two strong candidates who exceeded my requirements and expectations. I felt I should move quickly before competition for them escalated, and because I had an elevated target to meet.

Both candidates cruised through the interview process, as both women were polished, professional, and proven. Add to that the huge plus that they would be able to hit the ground running—this was crucial for me as I needed to minimize ramp time, considering our clock was ticking toward our fiscal year end and executive leadership expected results.

As I prepared the offer letters and reflected on the multiple conversations and interviews I had with each, something wasn't sitting well with me about my interactions with one of the candidates, Linda. Despite her exceptional credentials, she was verbose.

Her explanations and examples during interviews had gone on a bit too long, and she hadn't responded to the verbal and nonverbal cues from myself and others. Having had similar transgressions in the past myself, I quickly convinced myself this was something that could be overcome with coaching. And, after I expressed my intentions of making an offer, she felt compelled to continue to convince me, at length, that I was making the right decision. I quickly chalked it up to passion, energy, and excitement to join the team and contribute.

In reality, both issues pointed to a situational awareness problem, a concept I had experience with while playing quarterback at Oregon State in the late 80s. Good quarterbacks at the D1 level have acute situational awareness in order to recognize blitzes, alter pass protections, change plays at the line of scrimmage, or simply throw the ball away to keep a drive alive or avoid a turnover. Although situational awareness wasn't in the job description, in hindsight I knew it was critical for success at multiple levels in the organization. If hired, Linda would interface with internal and external customers consistently. Yet we were in the final stages of the hiring process, and I needed to move forward quickly. So, despite these seemingly minor red flags, I made the decision to go ahead with the hire instead of investigating these concerns further.

It ended up costing me.

Initial feedback was overwhelmingly positive as colleagues started to experience Linda's obvious strengths. But it didn't take long for the same red flags I saw to surface. A few months in, I realized the magnitude of my error. Under the pressure of goals, a desire to impress, colleague competition, and the need to achieve quickly, Linda's explanations grew *longer* under stress, adding to her intensity and verbosity. My coaching and personal experience in this area made little difference in curbing her behavior and its impact, thus costing me and our business dearly—with strained customer relationships, lost productivity, missed targets, challenges amongst my team, and questions from my senior leaders. I had to move her off my team and eventually out of the business.

The embarrassing and ironic part of this was that it was my own lack of situational awareness that prevented me from making the right adjustments prior to hiring. In the decades that have followed, I have come to zero in on the red flags that arise and slow the decision process down to take the additional steps necessary to vet through concerns. Hiring too fast, in my experience, has proven to be a risk I can't afford to take.

---

## WAITING TOO LONG TO FIRE

David Parsin, Vice President, North America, Artificial Solutions

**Managing** people can be messy. And I don't like messy.

I once used the miniature scissors on my Swiss Army knife to give a haircut to a friend. It took about two hours and involved three things that should have made for a disaster: a crazy swirl of wavy hair that had its way with my friend's head during his extended trip to Europe, a torrential rainstorm in Italy, and a little too much access to Italian wine prior to both the idea and execution of the cut. It took two hours because I like precision—*measure twice, cut once*—and also, I had never cut hair before. I should also mention that it took two hours for *just one side of his head.* I had another friend with another Swiss Army knife working the other side. This other "stylist" is more of an artist and showed great flair but less precision during *his* inaugural haircut and was done in about five minutes. Let the historical record show that the left side of his head, the side I was responsible for, proved to be the better cut for the friend and his head due to the care I took and the attention to detail I showed.

My love for detail started early and was validated and magnified when I enrolled at Stanford University. There, I played on the baseball team that won national championships in 1987 and 1988, in great part due to the precise execution of our practices, the study of the mechanics of the game, and the detailed analysis of the percentages and probabilities of the "game within the game." I majored in electrical engineering, which proved to be a great fit for me as success in that subject, like baseball, required logic, precision, and accuracy—three things that were essential later when I headed to Harvard for my MBA and, eventually, as I began my professional career.

As I graduated and joined the workforce, my attention to detail and passion for precision continued to serve me well as I worked as an individual contributor in a variety of technology organizations. Over time, though, my responsibilities grew and moved me away from the comfort of the binary technology and more toward the less comfortable and less precise responsibilities of leading people and managing teams. Managing talent in an organization, including hiring, giving regular constructive feedback, promotions, etc., all fall into varying shades of gray . . . colors I find messy!

Perhaps the messiest gray of all came when my job required me to move people out of the organization (aka, firing). I found myself wondering if I had given enough feedback to the employee prior to the termination conversation. Had I shared my disappointment with them regarding their work? Did I leave them alone to work their way through difficult situations instead of offering the guidance a good leader should? My degrees taught me little (if anything) about firing employees who did not perform or proved to be a poor fit. I was out of my league, and the mistakes started adding up.

Over the years, I discovered there were many reasons I conducted those end-of-employee life cycle issues poorly. The first was that I find confrontation uncomfortable. I am a pretty easy-going guy and manager; giving criticism doesn't come easily. Another reason was that I know what it takes to find replacements for key positions, especially during times when we enjoy a strong economy. Strong workers weren't always ready to leave their position, and there was great expense to bringing on a new employee. Would it have been easier just to keep who we had? I also knew that releasing an employee oftentimes brought drama that took its toll on the team. Would the team be strong enough to weather this type of big interruption? And, finally, firing felt like a confirmation of my own failures in hiring and managing this employee—something that was hard to admit.

Recently, it became clear that someone on my team needed to be released due to poor performance. My team was suffering because they had a colleague who wasn't a fit and wasn't doing his share of the work. As before, I began second-guessing the costs to removing him from the team and briefly considered delaying, this time due to the great demands on quarterly results and my fears that they would be in jeopardy. But I resisted the urge to delay and moved quickly. By cutting ties with appropriate speed, I freed up not only my time and my mindshare (this had been weighing on me heavily), but also that of the rest of my team. The team expressed relief about the change, and individual contributions picked up across the team to help us achieve our objectives.

As leaders, it is our responsibility to offer regular, customized feedback to each team member so there is the opportunity to grow within the workplace. But once it becomes clear a team member is not a good fit, the right thing to do is to make a swift extraction.

By taking immediate action in this instance, I demonstrated to the rest of my team not only that each of us would be held accountable for our actions and results, but that all of us would be validated for the good work, creativity, and resourcefulness we each brought to the team. Making a swift decision to release a poorly performing employee can demonstrate your willingness to do the difficult things you need to do as a leader to make the team better.

---

## LEADER SELF-ASSESSMENT

Please rate yourself as you believe your team members would rate you on the following skills and talents by choosing the appropriate number from the terms below. Then total the numbers to see your overall self-assessment for this category.

| LOUSY | NEEDING TO IMPROVE | OK | PRETTY GOOD | OUTSTANDING |
|---|---|---|---|---|
| 1 | 2 | 3 | 4 | 5 |

**Do I hire too fast or fire too slow?**

_______ 1. My team would say I am __________ at hiring people aligned to the company's purpose.

_______ 2. My team would say I am __________ at hiring people aligned to the company's values.

_______ 3. My team would say I am __________ at hiring with alignment to cultural fit.

_______ 4. My team would say I am __________ at taking the time necessary to get to know candidates before bringing them into the company.

_______ 5. My team would say I am __________ at extracting poorly performing team members in a reasonable amount of time.

________ **Hiring total**

---

23+ = Outstanding—this is a real strength for you
18–22 = Pretty good—you are on your way to greatness
13–17 = OK—not bad (but do you really want to be an average leader?)
8–12 = Needing to improve—you have some work to do
5–7 = Lousy—this is a real challenge for you and therefore, for your team

# MISTAKE #5

## FAILING TO GIVE AND SOLICIT FEEDBACK

YOU MISSED ALL OF YOUR GOALS.
BECAUSE OF POOR MANAGE-MENT.
I'LL GO INTO MORE DETAIL WHEN I DO MY 360-DEGREE REVIEW OF YOU.
I MEANT TO SAY YOU'RE DOING GREAT.
THAT'S WHAT I MEANT TO SAY TOO.
Dilbert.com DilbertCartoonist@gmail.com
5-29-14 ©2014 Scott Adams, Inc./Dist. by Universal Uclick

# FAILING TO GIVE AND SOLICIT FEEDBACK

Giving and receiving feedback is tough and uncomfortable. That's why most leaders and their teams don't do it very well, if at all.

When my peers from The Table Group and I work with teams, we do a pre-event assessment proprietary to The Table Group, which is cleverly named "The Team Assessment." It is based upon Patrick's best-known and best-selling book, *The Five Dysfunctions of a Team.* The Five Dysfunctions in order are:

**Absence of Trust**

**Fear of Conflict**

**Lack of Commitment**

**Avoidance of Accountability**

**Inattention to Results**

Almost without exception, the lowest score for a team the first time we work with them concerns that fourth dysfunction: Avoidance of Accountability. And giving and receiving feedback fits squarely in that category.

That practice is so important, in fact, that at the end of our first two-day off-site with executive teams, my peers and I run an exercise called *Team Effectiveness*. In this exercise, everyone on a team shares, in front of the group, one specific behavioral item each team member does well that they should keep doing, followed by one specific behavior they could improve upon. When we announce this exercise, most people at the off-site, who have not participated in this before, have a look on their face that suggests they wish they had not come back after the last break. The exercise is raw and a bit uncomfortable at first because most of us are not used to giving honest, direct feedback to one another, especially in front of a group.

But if done in the spirit of making the team better, and by keeping in mind that feedback is a gift, this approach to peer-to-peer feedback is extremely powerful. When my "class" at The Table Group ran through this exercise about four years ago at our own off-site, I had four of my five peers give me constructive feedback along these lines: "You know Mike, sometimes you might want to think before you speak." Four out of five! I said *thank you* and called my wife that night and shared the story and the feedback I received with her. She responded, "I've been telling you for *20 years* that you need to think before you speak! But your peers share it, and *now* you want to work on it?" Honest, direct, peer-to-peer feedback is truly powerful. Difficult without practice, but powerful and common among great teams.

But why is giving and receiving feedback so difficult? We know we need to do it, that our people deserve it, and that regular, direct feedback will make the team better. In fact, if we think about those best teams we have ever been a part of, in most instances the team was marked by honest and direct feedback, both when things went well and when they didn't.

## FAILING TO GIVE AND SOLICIT FEEDBACK

We all learned the importance of feedback early on. My kids' sports teams provide great examples:

My daughter, Elena, plays point guard for her high school and on a competitive club basketball team that travels the U.S. Her coaches give brutally honest feedback, so much so that my wife often leaves the gym where the team is playing because criticisms are instant and intense. Not only must my daughter take direct feedback from coaches, but she must give it repeatedly in her role as floor general. And she and her teammates must give and receive feedback to one another throughout the game if they are to perform at their best and get what they all want: a win.

My son, Jack, has recently tried his hand at lacrosse. Boise is an up-and-coming lacrosse hub with new teams being launched every month. In one year, the city has gone from 14 teams to 104! But lacrosse is not easy to understand without clear coaching and guidance. "Cradling" is an important skill, but the technique takes time to master and direct feedback is critical to getting it right. And hitting another player with your stick, something both primal and innate in every boy I have ever known, is legal but must be done in a certain way to avoid time in the penalty box. Boys new to the sport need constant feedback, not only from their coaches, but also from their more experienced teammates if they are to learn the game and have success on the field.

Even my 10-year-old, Gabs, who favors soccer, gives and receives feedback regularly on her team. She and her teammates have specific goals about juggling the ball and push each other to better results on a weekly basis. Even at 10, they know they must get 50,000 touches this summer or they will hear about it from their coaches and their teammates. How else will they get better and create a winning team?

But on a leadership or work team, as opposed to a field or court, for some reason it seems harder. It's not easy telling your employees or a colleague that their performance could have been better and how they might improve. Or telling your boss how he or she might have done things differently for the good of the team. Or asking someone who works *for* you what you might do better as a leader. And yet, we've seen continually that this is exactly what must happen for a team and organization to thrive.

As leaders, we must be willing to provide honest and direct feedback, sometimes publicly and at other times privately, when things go right and when they go wrong. As leaders, we must also insist our people give one another clear, candid feedback and perhaps most importantly, be willing to solicit feedback ourselves.

## FAILING TO PROVIDE RECOGNITION

Sanjay Mehrotra, President and CEO,
Micron Technology, Inc.

**Soon** after I joined Micron as CEO in 2017, I pulled my executive team together in Half Moon Bay, California, for a two-day off-site. Although I had spent time with everyone on the team individually and the team had been together as a full group for various meetings, I wanted to make sure our senior leadership team spent some extended time together in the first 90 days of my tenure. If the company was going to grow and succeed in achieving its lofty goals, this team would need to become a *great* team, and we needed to do it quickly. To get there, I knew the members of the team would need to get to know one another better and to become aligned both behaviorally and intellectually.

During the second day of the event, we had a discussion about the organization's core values, with the intention of communicating those values across the enterprise in the weeks ahead. As we worked together to finalize those core values, we went through an exercise where we individually thought of one person in the organization who was a great fit at Micron. Someone who we would not only enthusiastically rehire, but if we could find more people just like them, we would hire them as fast as we could. Then we listed the qualities that made them such a great fit. We took turns sharing with the rest of the group the names and characteristics of those we had listed.

As we wrapped up the exercise, we commented on how several people had been named multiple times in the exercise, and that one person's name was shared *four* different times. Our company has more than 34,000 employees! Our facilitator asked if the people on the list, especially those listed multiple times, were told often enough how important they were to the company.

It got quiet in the conference room.

My executive team is made up of extremely smart, analytical leaders who move fast and push hard to make sure we reach our organizational goals. As with many senior leaders in technology, and in other industries I suspect, we often move quickly to what's next and fail to slow down enough to celebrate success and thank the people in our organization when they do great things. I have been guilty of this too many times in my career, in spite of having great intentions to be better at recognition. I take pride in giving direct, real-time feedback, and have developed a reputation throughout my career for "telling it like it is" in individual conversations, team meetings, and presentations. I learned this first from my father, who was an extremely direct, driven man. He had high expectations, and if any of my three siblings or I needed constructive criticism, he was never shy about providing it.

I carried my father's ways into my career both at Intel—where the culture of *disagree and commit* reinforces it—and then at Sandisk, where I was a co-founder and CEO. The cultural diversity of the executive leadership team there led to a culture of feedback, honesty, and productive conflict. If I am honest with myself, though, I am more apt to offer that direct feedback when things go wrong or don't meet my expectations, than when they go well. This is something I knew I couldn't afford to have happen going forward at Micron. As the CEO of the organization, I know I need to find ways to do this better—that it starts with me—and needed to continue throughout my executive team.

And it did, in fact, start with me right then and there at the off-site. I picked up the phone and called the employee who had been named by four different executives. His name is Naga, and when his manager, Scott, our EVP of Technology, called him and he answered, Scott handed the phone to me. I put him on the speaker so we all could hear, and I said, "Naga, this is Sanjay. The senior executive team and I are at an off-site in California. We just went through an exercise where we listed employees that align perfectly to our core values. Your name came up several times by several different leaders, so we thought we'd call you as a group to make sure you know how valuable you are to the company. Thank you for all your great work and for exhibiting our values, the behaviors that make our company a great one." He said thank you, and the executive team spontaneously broke out in applause and cheers before we said goodbye, adding additional meaning and emotion to the effort to recognize him and his great work.

That call took about three minutes. A small, simple gesture that had real impact on a great employee. I learned later that Naga, although a bit embarrassed by the call, really appreciated it, told his family about it, and said it was a call he didn't think he would ever forget.

Part of being both a high-performing and healthy organization is having an engaged workforce, and a big part of that is making sure employees are appropriately recognized and appreciated for their great efforts. We can't make the mistake of assuming good people know their value. That needs to be demonstrated first by me and my executive leaders. My leaders throughout Micron need to take ownership and personal responsibility to make sure this is a company that recognizes great work, gives feedback when things go well, and celebrates our successes.

---

## FAILING TO FORCE HARD AND IMPORTANT CONVERSATIONS

Brian Smith, CEO and Principal,
DEANCO Management Group, Inc.

**"Hey,** Brian, do you have a minute? There is something I'd like to talk to you about *privately*." The question came from one of my direct reports. I'll call him Jacoby.

I've always been a fan of the "open door policy" and over the course of my career as a leader up to that point, I took any and all impromptu meetings ever requested. Good leaders do that, right? I had appreciated the individual time previous managers had spent with me throughout my career, and my sense was the best leaders practiced this policy by taking the extra one-on-one time, listening to their people, and solving the problems they faced with respect to their work.

As he entered my office for our one on one, Jacoby closed my door—a closed-door meeting as a result of an open-door policy. Funny. He had two things he wanted to share with me, the first being a business issue related to a struggle he was having with a supplier. He said he felt he had made a mistake and wanted to share it with me, but not in front of the team. This was something I had seen multiple times before, in fact, with this very same supplier, and had a pretty good idea how to solve it. The second thing on his mind concerned an issue with a colleague and was going to be a bit harder to solve. People issues, I have found, are usually trickier, and this was no exception. As Jacoby explained the situation I could see that it was a highly charged, emotional issue with another one of my directs. I'll refer to her as Annika.

What I should have done in this situation was to force Jacoby and Annika to have a hard conversation and share their feelings directly with one another. But I didn't. It turned out to be a time-wasting mistake, and one I had made countless times before. In fact, I had made this same mistake with these *same two* leaders multiple times in the past. Each time they had "issues" I would take their individual meetings, then I would listen and act as a sounding board for one or both of them *separately*, so I could then make some suggestions to remedy the situation. Occasionally, I would even go back and forth between them, again separately, to try to help them come to a resolution.

What I found over time was that their relationship never got better, and I was a big part of the problem. The two of them coming to me separately made *my* relationship with each of them better, but the relationship between *them* continued to suffer. Their issues not only kept them from establishing a good relationship, but it was distracting them and others from their work. Handling their issues individually took hours and hours, and that's time I'll never get back. I easily could have avoided this loss by having them give one another feedback directly and work it out on their own. I finally realized my mistake and pulled them together for a three-way, admittedly difficult conversation and told them I would no longer be available for these separate meetings. They would need to talk through issues they were having together first, and if there was no resolution, they could then come to me *together,* and I would make the final call.

With respect to the business issue Jacoby mentioned, I can say I handled that one better, at least this time. Having heard and addressed that same vendor issue before, I knew I had made a mistake the first time it came up months ago by not forcing a group conversation when it was originally brought up to me. This time, though, I gave Jacoby my initial thoughts and then asked him to share his mistake with our team at our weekly meeting the next day. When he did, another team member, I'll call her Petra, said she was facing the same thing with a different vendor and had made a similar error. By bringing it up in front of the group, not only did everyone benefit from and learn from the conversation, but the team came up with a better solution than I was going to suggest, had I kept the conversation with Jacoby private. The team also had an opportunity to see that being vulnerable and sharing a mistake is a great way to make the team better. Making sure this important conversation was held in front of the group helped the team and would save time down the road in similar situations.

Having been through these experiences and others like them over my years as a leader, I always look for ways to force difficult and important conversations between members of my team. Those hard conversations build relationships, make the team more cohesive, and, most importantly, lead to better business results.

## FAILING TO GIVE IMMEDIATE FEEDBACK

Kamal Aggarwal, Executive Vice President,
National Semiconductor, LSI Logic,
Fairchild Semiconductor (retired)

**By** the time I became the Executive Vice President at one of the world's leading semiconductor manufacturers, I had rightly earned the reputation of being a hard-ass. My colleagues and many in the technology industry knew that I was a straight shooter who always spoke the truth. No sugar coating. Ever.

Early in my career, all too frequently I saw a leadership error that I knew I couldn't allow myself to make. Many leaders avoided confrontation by allowing "stage-managed" results—results that were for show and hid problems and challenges in the business. They seldom encouraged bad news. I saw leaders failing to offer direct, immediate feedback to someone who was making a mistake, doing something that hurt the company, or was failing to keep his commitments. I saw this happen over and over. Leaders either were afraid to make waves, cared more about their popularity than company results, or planned to provide input at a later time. Those times often never came. Consequently, results were subpar. You often get what you are willing to accept if you don't demand accountability.

It became clear to me that this was not the way a good leader leads, and I was unwilling to repeat that same mistake. I had given my team one battle cry (reducing cycle time by 50 percent without sacrificing quality), and I needed them to ensure it happened. And, they needed leaders who gave honest, immediate feedback if we were ever offtrack. They also needed to know that a culture that accepted the same failing practices and approaches, one that made excuses or ignored promises, would no longer be tolerated.

A good leader needed to provide immediate, direct feedback that would improve both the performance of the employee and the results of the company. This was my primary goal. I felt it was why I was hired.

An example of this came soon after I took over as the Executive VP of Worldwide Operations at National Semiconductor. As I sat in a meeting with several other senior executives and the company plant managers, I saw that those managers were sheltering the executives from the truth of how the business was running. Things were not going well in the company, but executives were hearing a rosy tale that didn't match reality. This was helping no one, and this behavior was inhibiting the company from achieving its goals. The executive team needed to hear the honest, unfiltered truth and hear it immediately, so that we could turn things around.

As one particular plant manager told his fable regarding his area, I challenged him immediately and called him out publicly for his inaccurate information. This had not been a common practice at the company before my arrival, and the feedback, especially the public nature of that feedback, was embarrassing to him.

He called me afterwards, quite angry, and asked that I not do that again, especially publicly. I explained that if we were to become a high performing organization, our culture would have to embrace direct, honest feedback up and down the organization. And that the public nature of that feedback was critical. Had I not called him and others out publicly in that meeting for misinformation, it would have implicitly condoned that behavior, which then would propagate across the organization and get in the way of our success.

To his credit, he took the feedback to heart, made big changes with approach to feedback across his part of the organization. His results improved as did others' in the organization as together we embraced this concept. It helped us achieve our singular goal that year of reducing cycle time by 50 percent without sacrificing quality.

A change to the culture had begun. It required honest, immediate, often public feedback up, down, and across the organization. Cycle times improved, profits grew, employees started taking greater pride and held one another accountable, and our organization was a better one as a result.

## BEING CLOSE-MINDED TO TEAM FEEDBACK

Dr. John Slattery, Founder, Slattery Orthodontics

I knew from the day I met Kathy that our working relationship was not going to work out.

I had moved back to my hometown after spending over a decade in school, earning three degrees at three different universities on the path required to become an orthodontist. I had been hired into a large group practice with three other doctors and on that fateful first day was assigned Kathy—and only Kathy—as my lead clinical assistant, who would help me manage my practice within the practice. In addition to a practice at the main location, the two of us were charged with starting a satellite practice one day a week.

As we were introduced, we sized each other up. I had an image in my mind as to whom my first employee might be—and she wasn't it. If I had a panel of 10 or 15 people to interview, I doubt she would have been my first choice. I remember someone at the office letting me know that Kathy had worked in orthodontics for a long time and probably already knew more than I did. Was that threatening to me, a newly minted orthodontist? You bet it was. We were peers in age. She had a quiet confidence about how to do things and wasn't afraid to point out a mistake or how things *should* be done. I had expected to be the superior in position but was feeling minimized and threatened by her.

I'm sure my body language said a lot that day. I remember thinking to myself, "The last thing I need is someone telling *me* how to run *my* practice."

I couldn't have been more wrong.

In the previous 15 years, leading up to that first day, I had been at the bottom of a number of different hierarchies.

At Santa Clara University as an undergraduate, I studied mechanical engineering and every day was taught by professors telling me what I needed to know and giving honest guidance and feedback when I did something wrong. But I was learning a process and learning the practical ways to someday be an engineer. I was also on the crew team and every morning at 5 a.m. got on the water and listened to my coaches and coxswains (110-pound tyrants of the vessel who watched my every move alongside the other oarsmen) happily screaming at me when my timing was off. The idea was that this immediate and honest feedback would help us achieve the elusive "swing" (called being *in the zon*e in other sports) and help us avoid having to give up our shirts to our competitors in our next race, a humbling but motivating tradition in that sport. Again, I was learning a process, the practical application of which would result in better times and hopefully, races won.

After graduation, I spent a few years working for Andersen Consulting. In that business, there were clear roles and reporting relationships and I was at the bottom of the org chart as a new consultant. The company was known for their set of systems and processes and I needed to learn them and conform to them. I was subservient to the managers, senior leaders, and partners, who knew more than I and often told me, without my input, what assignments I would be taking on and in which city I would live for each assignment. With greater experience and knowledge, they would direct my work, critique my approaches and the quality of my work, and show me the proven processes and practical approaches regarding how to be successful in client interactions.

Although I worked hard and found success in these different environments, I found I wasn't fulfilled in my career choice. With some great guidance from a friend's parent who was a college counselor, I chose a very different path and attended dental school in California and orthodontic school in Philadelphia. Again, smarter and more knowledgeable people were telling me what I was—and wasn't—doing well. Looking over my shoulder in clinics and labs, my professors offered constant and critical feedback to get me where I needed to be as a professional and successful clinical practitioner in my trade.

After 15 years as the "low man on the totem pole," the one who *received* the feedback and had to do as others directed, I graduated from ortho school. Earning that diploma made me feel I should be *the* leader in all aspects of my practice. I had earned the degree, had all the appropriate clinical knowledge and training and now I was ready to be *the man*, the one in charge, and the one sole leader of my practice.

The problem with this, though, was that I was not skilled or experienced in actually *running* a practice. I knew the anatomy of the mouth, the mechanics of braces, the techniques, the angles, the tools that were necessary for fixing crooked teeth, overbites, and underbites, but I didn't know the practical components of running a successful practice including finances, billing, suppliers, appointment systems, or patient flow. These were the practical things I hadn't learned in school but desperately needed to be able to do well if my practice was going to succeed.

I suspect this is true for many rookie leaders—wanting to prove themselves as the one in charge and desiring to demonstrate their knowledge, competence, and smarts. With image and pride more important than they should be, these leaders are less open to ideas, insights, feedback on how to do things, and the strategies needed to be successful. It takes vulnerability to admit you need help, something I think is especially difficult for doctors and new leaders—and in my case, I was both.

As Kathy and I worked together over time, I came to recognize and appreciate her as a second key leader who was committed to the practice and shared my top priority: providing great care for our patients. When I allowed myself to be vulnerable and admitted to needing help, really needing Kathy (let's face it, probably more than she needed me), our working relationship improved, as did our practice. When I "got over myself" and opened myself up to listening to her wise counsel on the mechanics and the important systems and processes for running the business, we got better, and our business improved. I had the opportunity to focus on and use my key strengths, and trusted Kathy to use hers in support of our growing practice.

In fact, when I decided to leave that first partnership to start my own business, Kathy came with me and we launched the practice together. By taking advantage of the two distinct sets of skills and leveraging each of our strengths, we were able to create a successful new business. I recall the body language was much better on *that* first day.

Kathy and I have now been working together for almost 20 years. She still gives me honest, direct feedback, whether it be as we designed the building for our growing practice, when she has an idea for how to improve a system or process, or when there is a booger in my nose or broccoli in my teeth. (None of the nearly 70 patients I see in a given day want to see that!) Her direct feedback to me on these and other things results in a better work environment, happier employees, better care for our patients, and ultimately, a better, healthier business.

## FAILING TO SOLICIT FEEDBACK

Taavo Godtfredsen, Principal, TLG Associates;
CEO advisor, executive coach, and speaker

I like to think I am a pretty good husband and father. But being passionate about feedback and knowing that about 95 percent of people *think* they are self-aware* when only 10-15 percent truly are, I thought I would check my self-assessment and ask my family for some honest, direct feedback.

"How am I doing as a father and husband?" I asked each member of my family in individual conversations. "And, what's one thing I could do better?" I thought, believing I was in the 10-15 percent group, that there would be no surprises. Wrong!

I was happy that they all responded similarly to the first question and gave me a passing grade, but their responses to the second were very different. My wife responded that a bit more "chipping in" with some household tasks like garbage and recycling would be much appreciated. Fair criticism, and something I could absolutely do better.

My daughter had no comment on what I could improve upon when I asked a first time, but when I was persistent and asked again soon after, she told me that I could be more patient and not raise my voice as much. *Ouch*. Didn't see that one coming. I recognized the humor in my impatience when waiting for her response and thanked her for the constructive criticism. I agreed it was something I could do better as a father. I chalked that one up to something common that a lot of parents need to do better at.

My son's feedback was more immediate—and much more painful to hear. "Dad," he said, "you always interrupt me. You never let me finish what I am saying." *Double ouch.* That one really hurt, and I felt horrible. The last thing I want my son to feel is that I am not listening to him and valuing what he is sharing with me. I would interrupt him, thinking I knew what he was going to say. Talk about a parental blind spot—I had no idea I was doing this to him. Listening, as I have always felt strongly about, is what great parents and leaders do.

Having acknowledged and thanked them each for their feedback, I knew I had taken a good first step. But if this experience was going to truly be meaningful, if I was going to improve as a husband, father, and leader of my most important team, I knew I would not just have to listen and thank them, but I would have to make changes to my behavior.

I am extremely passionate about feedback, as it is the muscle behind continuous improvement. The idea behind feedback is really quite simple: How can we improve if we don't know how we are doing? As leaders, don't we want to model improvement and growth for our followers and demonstrate courage and humility? This is why I believe asking for feedback is the single biggest way a leader can have an impact on his or her organization. Now that's a bold statement to make and one that a number of the CEOs I have coached over the years have asked me to back up. While there is a wealth of data to support my position, one study by Zenger-Folkman supported it especially well.

Leveraging a database of more than 22,000 leaders and their completed 360 degree assessments, they took one item, "This person asks for and acts on feedback from others" to see how it correlated with a composite score for all of the items in their assessment.** This is what they discovered:

- Leaders in the top 10th percentile on "asking for and acting on feedback" were ranked in the 90th percentile of overall leadership effectiveness.
- Leaders in the 66th to 90th percentile on "asking for and acting on feedback" were ranked in the 71st percentile of overall leadership effectiveness.
- Leaders in the bottom 10th percentile on "asking for and acting on feedback" were ranked in the 12th percentile of overall leadership effectiveness.

Having worked with and interviewed hundreds of CEOs and executive leaders over the past two decades, my own qualitative research supports the importance of leaders asking for feedback as well:

- Multiple senior executives I have coached have made significant strides in their overall effectiveness and business outcomes, as reported by their peers and direct reports, after asking for feedback and taking action on that feedback. One of the most successful CEOs I have ever coached, for example, sent out a survey to the entire organization asking for feedback on his strengths (to amplify) and areas for improvement (to fix). Of course, when you ask for feedback, you set the expectation that you will do something with it—especially if you ask for it from all of your employees globally! This CEO did not disappoint. He first provided all of the employees with a summary of what he learned via video, approximately a week after sending the survey. He began the video perfectly, starting with "Everyone in the company gets a performance review, why shouldn't I?" He then methodically laid out his own performance plan for the coming year based on their input. This is what great leaders do. They don't preach about the importance of feedback, they model it. In this case, the CEO did it in the most powerful way possible.

- When the most senior leaders ask for feedback regularly, it sets the tone for other leaders to do the same and leads to continuous improvement for the whole organization. In many cases, people do what people see. It can be that simple!
- Also, by asking for feedback, a leader shows vulnerability, which allows others in his or her organization to do the same. This creates an environment of openness, sharing of ideas, and debate, and allows for better decisions and ultimately better organizational success.

I'll close with a simple question: What if every leader in your organization made a commitment to asking for feedback regularly and worked hard to change behaviors that the feedback recommended?

My own answer would be that your leaders would be more effective, business results would be more easily achieved, and your organizations would be stronger and healthier.

And those willing to apply that same approach at home would see better results there, as I am working to achieve as well.

*https://www.forbes.com/sites/jeffkauflin/2017/05/10/only-15-of-people-are-self-aware-heres-how-to-change/#4ebac69c2b8c

**https://www.forbes.com/sites/jackzenger/2015/02/12/the-question-that-improves-leader-effectiveness/#b5d0cc63df31

# LEADER SELF-ASSESSMENT

Please rate yourself as you believe your team members would rate you on the following skills and talents by choosing the appropriate number from the terms below. Then total the numbers to see your overall self-assessment for this category.

| LOUSY | NEEDING TO IMPROVE | OK | PRETTY GOOD | OUTSTANDING |
|---|---|---|---|---|
| 1 | 2 | 3 | 4 | 5 |

**Do I fail to give and solicit feedback?**

_______ 1. My team would say I am __________ at providing recognition for a job well done.

_______ 2. My team would say I am __________ at giving honest and direct feedback when things could improve.

_______ 3. My team would say I am __________ at giving immediate feedback.

_______ 4. My team would say I am __________ at being open to hearing unsolicited feedback from the team.

_______ 5. My team would say I am __________ at soliciting feedback from the team and acting upon it.

_______ **Feedback total**

---

23+ = Outstanding—this is a real strength for you
18–22 = Pretty good—you are on your way to greatness
13–17 = OK—not bad (but do you really want to be an average leader?)
8–12 = Needing to improve—you have some work to do
5–7 = Lousy—this is a real challenge for you and therefore, for your team

# CONCLUSION

I have been called a lot of things in my life.

Dad, Father, Daddy are three of my favorites. Three different names for the same role by my three kids. Not sure why, but my kids are all very different, and when they address me that way, even when it's to ask me for some cash, I love it.

My wife calls me a variety of things: Hubby, Darlin', Lover, and Willis (when I make that certain face—*Watchu talkin' 'bout, Willis?*) are some of the ones I like best from her. She has more colorful names for me as well.

Other favorites over the course of my 51 years include friend, uncle, buddy, amigo, neighbor, as well as a number of titles I have been honored to be called: leader, manager, boss, elder, captain, coach.

One thing I haven't been called as often as I'd like to report though, is *vulnerable*. This has been a challenge for me over the course of my life, especially in my roles as a leader. I started this book talking about my first role as a leader and some of the damaging mistakes I made. In the story I blamed the lack of guidance and lack of mentoring, and that definitely was part of it. But my own lack of humility and the arrogance I showed, especially in those first leadership roles, probably had even more to do with my many failures.

I know I'm not alone in being challenged in this area as a leader, but the truth is the very best leaders I have known and worked with are exactly that . . . vulnerable. They demonstrate it daily by saying things like *I'm sorry* or *I blew it* or *Help me* or *I'm not very good at this*. And when they admit their mistakes openly and honestly, the members of their teams and others in their organizations follow their lead. When leaders "go first" this way, their people can be more vulnerable as well, trust improves, and the team gets better. For great examples of vulnerability, you need not look any farther than the 25 stories on the previous pages in this book. Remarkable leaders admitting mistakes for the whole world to see. And for that I'm both in awe and forever grateful to them.

In the final mistake documented in this book, Taavo shared that a leader's ability to solicit feedback and then act on that feedback is so critical. I wholeheartedly agree, and I saved his story for last for a reason. Asking for raw, critical feedback is the ultimate demonstration of vulnerability. But the willingness to do it and act upon it ends up making leaders better, teams better, and organizations better. Its importance can't be overstated.

So, it is with feedback in mind that I offer a request and a challenge in wrapping up this book: The request is for feedback for me. One of the best things about writing a book about mistakes is that when you make them, and I surely have, you can put it to use for others to learn from. At #RookieMistakesBook, I invite you to tweet what I have left out or missed for the world to see and learn from. And I'll publish errors, omissions, and mistakes at Mike-McHargue.com as well as on my other social media platforms.

The challenge I offer is to assess your strengths and weaknesses as a leader through an assessment I have created with respect to the

25 mistakes referenced in this book. You probably noticed the assessment questions at the end of each section of the book, but they are all compiled in one larger assessment in the pages that follow to give you a chance to reflect on where your weaknesses are as a leader and what you may need to get better at for the good of your team and organization.

This assessment is available at Mike-McHargue.com also, and if you take it there, you get a fancy report back that addresses your areas of opportunity and provides some resources to help you get better. By taking it online, you also are given the opportunity to launch the same assessment to your team and ask *them* to rate *you* in the same areas, which will allow you to compare your self-assessment with that of your team. And the comparison report from that process is even fancier yet.

I wish you all the best as a leader. May you be vulnerable, ask for feedback, and learn from your mistakes as the best leaders do.

# LEADER SELF-ASSESSMENT

Please rate yourself as you believe your team members would rate you by choosing the appropriate number from the terms below. Then total the numbers for each section to see your overall self-assessment for each mistake category. This assessment is also available online at Mike-McHargue.com.

| LOUSY | NEEDING TO IMPROVE | OK | PRETTY GOOD | OUTSTANDING |
|---|---|---|---|---|
| 1 | 2 | 3 | 4 | 5 |

**Do I allow confusion?**

_______ 1. My team would say I am __________ at communicating the company's purpose.

_______ 2. My team would say I am __________ at communicating the company's values.

_______ 3. My team would say I am __________ at communicating the company's and team's goals.

_______ 4. My team would say I am __________ at communicating the company's and team's priorities.

_______ 5. My team would say I am __________ at continuously communicating the most important things in our business.

_______ **Confusion total**

| LOUSY | NEEDING TO IMPROVE | OK | PRETTY GOOD | OUTSTANDING |
|---|---|---|---|---|
| 1 | 2 | 3 | 4 | 5 |

**Do I fail to connect with my team?**

_______ 1. My team would say I am __________ at being open and vulnerable.

_______ 2. My team would say I am __________ at getting to know the members of the team.

_______ 3. My team would say I am __________ at listening.

_______ 4. My team would say I am __________ at giving them the right amount of guidance and support (not too much and not too little) for the team to succeed.

_______ 5. My team would say I am __________ at expressing gratitude.

________ **Connection total**

**Do I run truly awful meetings?**

_______ 1. My team would say I am __________ at ensuring clarity about our meetings.

_______ 2. My team would say I am __________ at starting meetings with clarity.

_______ 3. My team would say I am __________ at allowing for productive conflict in our meetings.

_______ 4. My team would say I am __________ at ensuring clarity of decisions, commitments, and actions during meetings.

_______ 5. My team would say I am __________ at ensuring we leave meetings with clear messaging.

________ **Meetings total**

## LEADER SELF-ASSESSMENT

| LOUSY | NEEDING TO IMPROVE | OK | PRETTY GOOD | OUTSTANDING |
|---|---|---|---|---|
| 1 | 2 | 3 | 4 | 5 |

**Do I hire too fast or fire too slow?**

_______ 1. My team would say I am __________ at hiring people aligned to the company's purpose.

_______ 2. My team would say I am __________ at hiring people aligned to the company's values.

_______ 3. My team would say I am __________ at hiring with alignment to cultural fit.

_______ 4. My team would say I am __________ at taking the time necessary to get to know candidates before bringing them into the company.

_______ 5. My team would say I am __________ at extracting poorly performing team members in a reasonable amount of time.

________ **Hiring total**

**Do I fail to give and solicit feedback?**

_______ 1. My team would say I am __________ at providing recognition for a job well done.

_______ 2. My team would say I am __________ at giving honest and direct feedback when things could improve.

_______ 3. My team would say I am __________ at giving immediate feedback.

_______ 4. My team would say I am __________ at being open to hearing unsolicited feedback from the team.

_______ 5. My team would say I am __________ at soliciting feedback from the team and acting upon it.

________ **Feedback total**

## TOTALS SUMMARY

Insert scores and totals here for each of the five assessment sections.

| | Confusion | Connection | Meetings | Hiring | Feedback |
|---|---|---|---|---|---|
| 1. | ______ | ______ | ______ | ______ | ______ |
| 2. | ______ | ______ | ______ | ______ | ______ |
| 3. | ______ | ______ | ______ | ______ | ______ |
| 4. | ______ | ______ | ______ | ______ | ______ |
| 5. | ______ | ______ | ______ | ______ | ______ |
| **Totals:** | ______ | ______ | ______ | ______ | ______ |

## ASSESSMENT RESULTS

23+ = Outstanding—this is a real strength for you
18–22 = Pretty good—you are on your way to greatness
13–17 = OK—not bad (but do you really want to be an average leader?)
8–12 = Needing to improve—you have some work to do
5–7 = Lousy—this is a real challenge for you and therefore, for your team

# ACKNOWLEDGMENTS

My smokin' hot wife and editor, Anna, has been editing books, over 300 of them at last count, for more than 30 years. For several of those years, I was on the board of a small publishing company and, in recent years, became an adviser to a boutique publishing firm, Aloha Publishing, near my home in Boise, Idaho.

So, for some time now, everything I needed to write a book was ready and waiting for me minus one key item: an author who was smart enough, indeed expert enough at a topic, to write something that anyone would find useful and want to read. Plus, my wife continually shared with me that writing a book is not only difficult but requires long periods of focus and great attention to detail—definitely not my strengths. Some people, she said, simply aren't cut out for it. I *knew* I was one of them, at least until I was struck by the notion that I do know a lot about one thing and have true, expert-level experience at it: making mistakes!

Whether anyone would want to read it is another matter and remains to be seen, but it appears at least *you* did. So, thank you for that.

There are times you should listen to your wife; her comments about how difficult it is to write a book turned out to be true. Not only was it difficult, but it also required the proverbial village to make it happen correctly. I am so grateful to my tribe of contributors, including the hundreds of executives I interviewed for this book over the past several years and especially the 25 who were vulnerable enough to allow me to share their stories here.

My team of book people included Molly McBride, Kim Thuleen, and Amy Hoppock, whose ideas and excitement seemed never ending. I also am grateful to my publisher, Maryanna Young, who encouraged me to bring this book to life.

Many thanks also go to Leslie Hertling, who turned my cover ideas into a work of art. Thanks for saving the day, Leslie! I also am indebted to the designers at Fusion Creative Works and to the team at Stoltz Marketing, including Katherine Johnson, Lacy Hopkins, and Kate Holgate, who helped me launch my work into the market.

And, thank goodness for the word people! This book could have been a real mess without the help of my editors and proofers: Anita Stephens, Dave Troesh, Jennifer Regner, and the editing team at Words With Sisters. Your work is tireless, painstaking, and often thankless, but I so appreciate you.

Thanks so much to my friends and colleagues at The Table Group. I'm especially grateful to Patrick Lencioni and Jeff Gibson, who have graciously mentored me over the last several years as I worked to craft my skills in the profession that feels like home. And to Al Amador and David Ross who took me under their collective wing as I started and built my business—I'm forever grateful for your guidance. And to my Principal Consultant comrades, especially in our West Pod—your collaboration and feedback is so appreciated.

I'm so very thankful for my super supportive family, starting with Anna, who was the glue that held this project (and me!) together from start to finish. I love you, darlin', you are *SS!* I also want to thank my three amazing kids, Elena, Jack, and Gabriella, who suffered greatly, having to hear idea after idea at dinner each night and on vacations and first thing in the morning and last thing at night. And I would be nowhere without my parents Lanita Allen and Mike McHargue and stepmom Liz McHargue. Your love and support of me and my crazy dreams are something I can never thank you enough for, and I try to pay forward with my own kids.

And, finally, to Jesus, the ultimate example of vulnerability. He really should be the first and the last on this list.

# ABOUT THE AUTHOR

Mike McHargue is a Principal Consultant with Patrick Lencioni's Table Group. He and his consulting team are part of the global movement to bring organizational health into our businesses. Over the last several years, his clients have included Micron Technologies, Carnival Corporation, Intel, Rio Tinto, World Vision, Applied Materials, Mutual of Omaha, Griffin Communications, St. Luke's Health System, and Apex Leaders, to name only a few.

Mike lives in Boise, Idaho, with his wife, Anna, and their three children, Elena, Jack, and Gabriella.

For more information regarding his work and The Table Group, contact Mike at mike.mchargue@tablegroupconsulting.com or visit his webpage at Mike-McHargue.com